Cultivating Lifelong *Faith*

Cultivating Lifelong *Faith*

True Stories of
Encounters with God That
Transform Lives

COMPILED BY
Gabriela Banks

Wheelbarrow Press

Cultivating Lifelong Faith

www.GabrielaBanks.com
Published by Wheelbarrow Press

Printed in the United States of America.
ISBN 978-1-7342668-0-1 (paperback)
ISBN 978-1-7342668-1-8 (eBook)

Cover and interior design: Gabriela Banks
Cover photos: vineyard by Jill Wellington; grapes in hands by Mythja Photography
Interior photos: vineyard by Jill Wellington, grapes by Aalmediah from Pixabay

---

NOTE: Some names and identities have been changed for privacy purposes. In these cases, identifying details may have been altered, but the essence of the story has been preserved to convey the transforming love of Jesus Christ. Editors have done their best to maintain each team member's unique voice in the editing process.

All proceeds of this book will be donated to King City outreach programs.

For my PBCC church family
and all who long for
more of God's presence in their lives

They have conquered [the accuser of our brothers]
by the blood of the Lamb
and by the word of their testimony.
—Revelation 12:11

Contents

Foreword

From the first moment I met Gabriela (Gabi) Banks, I immediately sensed a woman in love with God, full of enthusiasm and burning with desire to be light and serve her Savior. It wasn't long before she began telling me about her book project documenting extraordinary stories about God's love and tangible presence on mission trips to King City, California.

A few weeks later, I began reading a draft of the manuscript you now have in your hands. I remember very well the first time I read *Cultivating Lifelong Faith.* It didn't take long for me to get hooked. I've read it three times. Why? How is it possible a stack of pages with a series of stories can be so engaging and inspiring? Well, I found the answer! And I hope you, my beloved reader, after reading this book, will discover and experience what God can do—not only in King City, but in your own life.

For over 40 years, I have had the privilege of serving as a pastor in Ciudad Juarez in the state of Chihuahua, Mexico, which lies on the U.S. border adjacent to El Paso, Texas. My first 29 years as a pastor were glorious. But things happened for the most part within the four walls of my church. Then something extraordinary happened. The Holy Spirit intervened in a profound way, giving me clear instructions to leave the church I loved and start a new stage in my life. Although it was difficult to leave the precious people of that congregation, I obeyed the Lord, entrusting them to an excellent team of pastors who have continued the work God gave me the privilege to begin when I was 18 years old. Then in 2002, God instructed me to fast and pray for my city for 21 days in a public park.

Here is where I identify with Gabi and Peninsula Bible Church Cupertino. *Cultivating Lifelong Faith* is a powerful book, not only for the stories themselves, but for the testimony of how a congregation leaves its four walls and initiates the glorious process of shepherding a city. That was exactly my experience in Ciudad Juarez.

During the 21-day fast in the park, a newspaper reporter came to me thinking I was a mad man on a hunger strike. I told him I wasn't protesting but learning how to love my city and asking God to bless it. The reporter came back each day to ask me what God was saying so he could publish it in the newspaper the next day. As news spread that a pastor was praying for the city, people started coming to the park asking for prayer—prostitutes, drug dealers, housewives, professionals, business people, and government leaders, including those from the State Capital 320 kilometers away. Following the last day of the fast, 4,000 people gathered at the park to pray for the city!

After this, God opened the door for us in one of the most corrupt prisons in the city. Under the authority of the mayor of Ciudad Juarez, we took over the prison, instilled kingdom principles, and then observed its transformation. The number of inmates who gave their lives to Christ increased dramatically, and this prison is becoming one of the best prisons in the entire Mexican Republic. We rejoice in this and are continually surprised by the extraordinary things God wants to do through ordinary people like all of us.

After this exciting adventure, the Holy Spirit gave us the following word: *"Just as it happened in the prison, so it will happen in the city."* We were overjoyed to hear this. But later we understood that, just as the prison was labeled one of the worst in the nation, so the city would also be named, "The Murder Capital of the World." God, in his magnificence and majesty, was setting the stage for what we call today, "The Miracle of Juarez." Just 18 months after receiving this dishonorable title, violence had decreased by 93%, showing the whole world what God can and wants to do in our cities and nations! This was just the beginning.

I am fully convinced that *Cultivating Lifelong Faith: True Stories of Encounters with God That Transform Lives* describes exactly this—God transforming lives though personal encounters that build faith! Fabulous to read, these stories allow us to feel as though we were physically present, witnessing the wonders of God with each and every one of the protagonists, both the volunteers and those being served.

How can we not identify with Thomas (Chapter 6) as he loses his insecurity and enters sheer joy as he carries Miguelito on his shoulders, later discovering the powerful influence he had on this four-year-old's entire family?

How can we not feel the presence of God when Hannah's relationship with Jesus Christ (Chapter 8) is impacted through her interaction with little Brittany?

How can we ignore the challenge George (Chapter 10) faced as he sacrificed his time on the varsity volleyball team to love underprivileged children like Paco and his two little sisters and five small cousins?

How can we not understand the vital importance of being a father and having a father when young Alicia sees in Jano the father figure she never had (Chapter 11)?

How can we not get teary-eyed and feel compassion as we read Gail's bittersweet story (Chapter 15) of meeting Doris and finding out that Tracy, Doris' 10-year-old daughter, was diagnosed with cancer?

I could continue commenting about Sophia (Chapter 22), Esther (Chapter 12), and Shea (Chapter 4), on the riches of the affirmation circles (Chapter 13), the miracles of the climate changes (Chapter 14), the fire at Whisper Canyon (Chapter 17), and other experiences where God's power and glory were manifested. Through these stories, I received glorious blessings as I delighted in *Cultivating Lifelong Faith.*

Now it is up to you, my beloved reader, to begin the amazing journey through each page, each story, each testimony, and above all, each person's heart. As you read, I pray you will experience God's amazing love. I pray you will come to know his desire to transform cities and nations. I pray you will discover how simple and powerful it is to believe God and give our time and resources to love our neighbor.

I celebrate the vision, discipline, perseverance, faith, and above all, the love of this woman in love with God, full of enthusiasm and burning with desire to be light and serve her Savior—Gabi Banks—for her obedience and determination to produce and deliver this invaluable gift, *Cultivating Lifelong Faith.*

Pastor Poncho Murguía
Director, Transform Our World, Mexico
"His grace is sufficient"

I. WATER INTO WINE

This [water now become wine],
the first of his signs,
Jesus did at Cana in Galilee,
and manifested his glory.
And his disciples believed in him.
—John 2:9, 11

Chapter 1

Encounters with God Transform Lives

It's one thing to read about God parting the Red Sea to free his people from slavery, defeating enemy armies with a praise band, or Jesus healing a leper in an instant (Exodus 14; 2 Chronicles 20:20-23; and Mark 1:40-45). But it's a game-changer when you have a personal encounter with the living God.

Experiencing God's tangible presence changes everything.

That's what's happening as teens and adults from Peninsula Bible Church Cupertino (PBCC) and Willow Glen Bible Church (WGBC) encounter the Lord on mission trips to King City, a hard-working agricultural community in Central California. God is becoming real to us and transforming our lives. We then turn around and show love to the people of King City, and he transforms them, too.

The funny thing is, on my first few mission trips to King City, I thought we were just playing games and singing silly songs with kids. I had no idea our actions were actually changing the spiritual atmosphere of their city. It turns out that the components of this mission trip help facilitate these transformations.

This transformation work is easy because Jesus' love is contagious. As we plan a Vacation Bible School (VBS) program and women's crafts, we turn our affections to God, love one another and the people of King City, and watch God orchestrate the rest. We're simply walking into what God is already doing.

What's he doing, you ask?

Pretty much the same thing he did 2000 years ago—transforming hearts. When he performed his first miracle in Galilee, Jesus amazed his followers by doing something no one had ever seen before—he transformed plain water into exquisite wine. In so doing, Jesus revealed his true identity as the Son of God, the supreme authority over all of creation.

Several stories in this book show how Jesus is still astounding us today, transforming our plain and broken lives day by day into his flawless image. And in so doing, the King of kings is revealing *our* new identity as God's beloved sons and daughters, his heirs, his friends, a royal priesthood (Galatians 4:7; Romans 8:14-19; John 15:15; and 1 Peter 2:9).

Being from Silicon Valley or King City may help describe us, but it doesn't define us. Neither does how much money we have, what size house we live in, our education, our accomplishments, or our past mistakes, no matter how big.

The more we share life and build relationships with families in King City, the more those false identity markers and our cultural differences fade, and the more we step into our true identities as brothers and sisters in Christ, sons and daughters of the King.

God's Long-term Vision for King City and Beyond

This King of kings is on the move. The true stories described in this book are just the beginning of God's transforming work through the ministry in King City. He also has a plan to reclaim this city. This long-term vision isn't just wishful thinking—God impressed this on my spirit with a Bible verse and then confirmed it supernaturally with my iPhone.

During a quiet time, I was reading Isaiah 43:6-7, which was spoken by the prophet Isaiah concerning Israel and describes God's vision for the sons and daughters of the whole earth.

I will say to the north, Give up,
and to the south, Do not withhold;
bring my sons from afar
and my daughters from the end of the earth,
everyone who is called by my name,
whom I created for my glory,
whom I formed and made." —Isaiah 43:6-7

All of a sudden, these words jumped off the page and captured my full attention. I felt God was using these verses to speak directly to me about King City.

I instantly remembered something a King City pastor had said in a sermon eight months earlier. He explained that refugees from Mexico and Central America had been fleeing north into California for years to escape poverty, famine, and violence. Unfortunately, some of them brought violence with them, and by 2010 there was a clear division in California between the gangs of *the north* and the gangs of *the south.* Because of King City's central location in California between rival gang territories, their young people are often lured into gangs.

By God's grace, in the 11 years we've been attending this trip, we've never seen any signs of this while we're there. King City has always been peaceful when we've come to visit. But what surprised me the most was hearing the King City pastor describe how our spiritual influence is transforming and blessing their city.

So when I read Isaiah 43:6-7 that day, I immediately sensed God was giving me his vision for his sons and daughters involved in gangs, not only those in King City, but also those throughout California. I sensed him saying that he himself is making a way for his sons and daughters who are caught up in gangs to be set free and fully restored. The Lord wants to redeem gang members just as much as he wants to set *all* his sons and daughters free. *All* people are created in God's image for the purpose of giving him glory. *No one* has drifted too far from God to receive his blessings—this restoration is available to *any*one who believes in Jesus.

Two months later, the way God confirmed this vision with my iPhone freaked me out. I had been struggling for weeks to write this introduction, writing and erasing every sentence I wrote, uncomfortable with *my* ideas. I yearned to collaborate with God, but I wasn't hearing him clearly. When I asked a pastor for guidance, he encouraged me to read the book of Habakkuk, go to a high place, and take time to listen to the Lord as Habakkuk had done (Habakkuk 2:1).

The next day, I drove to the top of Mount Hamilton with my Bible and journal and spent the entire day with God. I prayed as I looked out over the San Francisco Bay Area and the Central Coast of California. I texted my husband and kids, asking them to pray for me to hear from God about what to write.

I wish I could say clouds parted and I heard God's clear voice. But I didn't. At the end of the day, I drove down the mountain frustrated, fighting off thoughts that I'd wasted an entire day.

Of course, I knew in my heart I hadn't, but couldn't help but feel disappointed.

Two days later it happened. On January 30, 2019, after spending an hour worshiping God, I was standing at the kitchen counter preparing a bowl of yogurt and blackberries for breakfast. Suddenly, my iPhone, which I had set face down on the counter, turned itself on and started playing worship music. Adrenaline shot through my body sending chills up and down my arms and legs. Sensing the Lord's presence in the kitchen with me, I instinctively took two steps back and knelt on the floor in total reverence to him.

God, what are you doing?

I'd given him permission years ago to use my electronic devices to communicate with me, telling him he could choose the songs that came up on my playlist. So when I hear lyrics that say just what I need to hear, I smile, thanking God for comforting me. But the way he spontaneously turned on my iPhone that day shattered all my expectations about how he can speak to us.

After about a minute of kneeling on the kitchen floor, I stood up and tuned my ears to the lyrics, thinking he was trying to speak to me with my iPhone. (And no, it was not my Australian Siri dude—I had not activated him.) I turned the phone face up and noticed the song playing was "There is a Name"[1] from Bethel Music's Victory album.[2] I set the phone down, quickly opened up my journal, and took notes. I watched and listened as six more songs from that album played in random order. After seven songs, the music stopped on its own.

The words that struck me from "There is a Name" were about prodigal sons and daughters returning home to God, which immediately reminded me of the Isaiah 43 passage. At that point, I knew Father God was confirming the vision he'd given me of his desire to bring his sons and daughters out of the gangs of the north and south. This connection felt stronger than a mere coincidence and resonated deeply in my spirit. While pondering over my notes, the lyrics that stood out to me from the seven songs proclaim that:

- God, whose power surpasses all other power on earth and in heaven, redeems prodigal sons and daughters ("There is a Name");
- God's promises are absolutely trustworthy ("Promises Never Fail");[3]
- Nothing, not a huge canyon or even death can separate us from the Lord because his triumph over the cross breaks chains that bind us ("Living Hope");[4]
- Although shame tries to keep us locked up in the grave, through his resurrection, Jesus, our Redeemer, sets us free ("Ain't No Grave");[5]
- God is *always* faithful to us ("Goodness of God");[6]
- Prison walls will shake because God's name is always victorious ("Victory Is Yours");[7] and
- One day every voice will sing endless praises to our all-powerful and compassionate God ("Endless Hallelujah").[8]

When I told my husband, an engineer and tech expert who worked at Apple for 14 years what had happened, he said, "Pretty cool! Siri is disabled when iPhones are face down. iPhones can't play music by themselves."

I tell you this story for two reasons. First, we need to know what God is saying because he often asks ordinary people like you and me to partner with him in his redemptive work. Knowing God's plans helps us join him in accomplishing his kingdom purposes to make sure our agenda lines up with his.

Second, we need to know what God is saying because what he says *will* come to pass. Whatever he speaks, he does (Isaiah 46:11; 55:11)! Therefore, if what I sensed about the Lord rescuing his sons and daughters from gangs is a true word from God, then *he* will deliver them. It won't be done by human power or strength, but by his Spirit (Zechariah 4:6). *He* will do it.

As a matter of fact, God is already at work redeeming his sons and daughters who are involved in gangs.[9] (See this footnote to find out how God is fulfilling this promise through a different PBCC outreach group.)

God guides his people in bringing his kingdom to earth, and we hear him best when we are abiding in him and in his Word. He is already going before us in King City. Over the past 11 years, we've seen how our simple offering of Bible stories, crafts, games, and songs is the plain water Jesus is using to create fine wine. We accomplish his kingdom purposes by continually asking him how we can join him in what he's already doing.

How God Lured Me into Serving in King City

Sometimes even when we don't ask, God is the one who pulls us into what he's doing. For example, because I'm tall, light-skinned, and don't have an accent, most people have no clue I'm 100% Mexican. For years, I took advantage of this, purposely hiding my Latina identity to avoid being discriminated against. I felt safer blending in with the *gringos* and never felt called to serve the Latino population. That is until God led me to PBCC.

My family and I became part of the PBCC family in the summer of 2001. In those early years, my spirit would come alive whenever I'd watch a presentation of the youth group's Mexicali mission trip during a Sunday service.[10] The Mexicali slideshows reminded me of childhood road trips. Dad would drive our station wagon out of Texas flatlands and over the mountains of Mexico where we'd visit our aunts, uncles, and cousins. My paternal grandfather was known for acts of service such as feeding the hungry in his own home even when he had no money. "Dios dirá," he would say. *God will say*. When he saw teen gang members standing on street corners, he'd invite them to church. My parents also modeled serving the needy in our low-income Latino neighborhood in Dallas, Texas.

So when I saw PBCC teens and adults hugging and loving Mexicali children, everything inside me tingled with excitement and I silently declared, *I want to be a part of this!* Unbeknownst to me, God was changing my heart and reconnecting me with my ancestral roots.

At the time, I was a stay-at-home mom with children ages one, three, and six, so I suppressed my enthusiasm, knowing I'd have to wait. Fourteen years later, when our youngest child was 15, I finally joined the team. Even though the outreach trip had moved from Mexicali to King City, I was still excited to serve the Latino population there. I've loved getting to know the people of King City and am so excited to share these testimonies of how God is transforming the hearts of those who serve on these trips.

Sharing Testimonies Transforms Your World

The testimonies[11] you are holding in your hand are extremely significant. In Bible times, sharing God-moments was a vital part of every character's walk with God. It was so important that God commanded the patriarchs in the Old Testament to celebrate feast days and keep memorials throughout their generations so the LORD's mighty acts would be remembered (Exodus 12:14 and Joshua 4:6-7, 24). Because of this command to remember Gods deeds, the Bible is the greatest collection of testimonies ever written. It's filled with story after story of broken people recounting not only what God did for them, but also how he partnered with them to bring heaven to earth in crazy-amazing ways.

But guess what? Remembering God's deeds wasn't just an ancient tradition for people in Old Testament times. It's equally important for us, too. (To learn how testimonies can transform your world, be sure to read Appendix B, "The Life-Changing Power of Sharing Testimonies.") The problem is, many of us aren't used to sharing our God stories. I hope by reading these testimonies, you'll taste and see God in your own life and sense his presence with you so you too can be transformed into his image. I pray you'll be inspired to share and celebrate God-moments with others. Spreading the good news of Jesus is a great way to shine his light to others.

The next chapter describes the structure of PBCC's King City outreach program so that as you read the testimonies, you'll understand how the components of the program help cultivate lifelong faith in teenagers.

Chapter 2

Cultivating Lifelong Faith: Components of the Trip

While writing this book, I discovered alarming research from Barna Group, which shows that 64% of U.S. young adults who went to church regularly and identified themselves as Christians "dropped out of church at some point during their 20s—many for just a time, but some for good."[12]

Although I was shocked to hear this, I was relieved to learn that researchers are also studying what keeps young people connected to God and their faith communities. Fuller Youth Institute (FYI) has conducted comprehensive studies on youth ministries and discovered many factors they believe foster long-term faith in young people.[13]

It just so happens that the structure of PBCC's youth group outreach program, designed nearly 40 years ago, includes key elements identified by FYI researchers for building and nurturing lifelong faith. The framework for PBCC's King City mission trip was developed in 1981 by Pastor Gary Vanderet, who has always had a passion for cultivating community. The elements Gary and others incorporated were intentionally designed not just to serve those in need but to disciple students in their relationship with the Lord, help them discover their gifts, and cultivate close intergenerational relationships. This program was originally implemented in Mexicali, Mexico and then passed down to pastors who moved the trip to King City in 2008.

Here are some of the components of PBCC's King City mission trip that FYI researchers say contribute to lifelong faith:

- Community-building activities such as sharing personal testimonies, affirming one another, and meeting in small groups enable students to develop strong relationships with pastors, adults, and other teens.
- A retreat program for teens encourages them grow in their relationship with Jesus, and a beautiful outdoor environment facilitates encounters with him.
- Youth pastors and adult team leaders disciple students in small groups and one-on-one as needed.
- Older students serve younger students, building relationships with them, both at PBCC and in King City.
- Students have several opportunities to grow in leadership.
- Teens and adults serve alongside one another and worship together in a multigenerational community.

These elements, described in this chapter and throughout the book, are powerful ways for our kids to connect with God, youth pastors, adults, and one another.

Barna Group has also done extensive research for over a decade to learn more about young people who stay connected to God and their faith communities.[14] Their book *Faith for Exiles,*[15] written by David Kinnaman and Mark Matlock, describes common characteristics that set "resilient disciples" apart from church dropouts. They define resilient disciples as Christians who go to church, trust God's Word, are committed to Jesus, and want to use their faith to impact society.

Two of the gems Kinnaman and Matlock discovered are that these twenty-somethings (1) had a transformational experience with Jesus which allows them to experience deep intimacy with him, and (2) they have developed meaningful intergenerational relationships with people who care for them spiritually.

As you will read in this collection of testimonies, students (and adults) who engage in the King City mission trip are also having these types of transformative and intergenerational experiences. That's not to say we're doing everything perfectly. On the contrary, there is so much more we can learn from Kinnaman and Matlock, FYI, and others about how to nurture spiritual growth in teens as well as adults. I highly recommend *Faith for Exiles* and FYI's research for parents, youth pastors, and anyone interested in helping others grow spiritually.

Key Components of PBCC's King City Mission Trip

I was so confused the first time I walked into the youth room during a King City prep meeting. High school students were laughing and chatting as they rummaged through boxes of costumes and craft supplies scattered all over the floor. Even though they knew what they were doing, it looked like sheer chaos to me. I offer this overview to give you the big picture of what we do and why we do it.

This overview will also help you see how the structure of this trip helps cultivate community and stimulates spiritual growth in teens as well as adults.

The overall goal of the trip is to love God and love people, both those in our own church community and in King City.

Two Locations: Whisper Canyon & King City

During our weeklong service trip, our team camps at Whisper Canyon Christian Campground, located in the foothills of California's Central Coast. This beautiful, rustic place has been bathed in prayer and worship for many years. At Whisper Canyon, heaven touches earth more noticeably than in the frenzy of Silicon Valley. We sense Jesus' presence and hear his voice during worship at the canyon circle, on hikes to the cross, or in huddle groups by the campfire. As you will read in these stories, many students have sensed the Lord's presence or heard his voice for the first time at Whisper Canyon.

For four days during that week, teams of students and adults pile into minivans and SUV's and drive through country roads into King City. We provide VBS programs to four churches in various locations.

Three Components of the Trip

There are three main parts of this yearly trip: (1) leadership training through student-led service, (2) ministry *to* students, and (3) an adult-led women's craft ministry.

All three of these elements help foster connections with Jesus and one another.

1. Leadership Training through Student-led Service

This program is designed for PBCC students in grades eight through twelve. The overall goal of the outreach portion of the trip is to be the loving hands and feet of Jesus as we share the gospel message to children and adults in King City.

Students have opportunities to grow in leadership by being in charge of different components of the King City VBS program, applying to be a student team leader (STL), and leading worship.

VBS Program. With adult supervision, students take the lead in delivering a VBS program for school-aged children. One month before the trip, the youth group meets at PBCC for training meetings to plan out these activities. Students are assigned to small groups to organize all the materials needed for the skits, memory verses, crafts, playground games, and sports camps at various locations in King City. At training meetings, students rehearse Bible story skits, create activities to help King City children memorize Bible Verses, assemble crafts related to the Bible stories, and organize the sports camps. That's what students were doing with those boxes on the floor!

Student Team Leaders (STLs). Students have the option of applying to be a student team leader at one of the sites in King City. With adult supervision, these students lead their peers in organizing skits, crafts, and memory verses. They're also responsible for setting the tone and being a role model for younger students. Being an STL is a wonderful opportunity for students to grow in leadership.

Worship. A small group of students leads daily sing-alongs for the VBS program as well as worship songs for nightly evening programs at Whisper Canyon. Being on the worship team is another opportunity for students to grow in leadership and in their gifts.

2. Ministry *to* Students

In addition to serving others, time is set aside for students to be spiritually fed each day. Students who volunteer on this outreach trip receive love, care, and guidance from youth pastors and adult leaders.

Sharing Testimonies and Receiving Prayer. Time is set aside during planning meetings for students and adults to get to know one another better. Every student shares their testimony of where they are on their faith journey. Because students are encouraged to be vulnerable in their sharing, tears are often a part of this experience. Adult leaders or other students take time to pray for those who shared their stories. Everyone then transitions to large group games, which foster lots of laughter among team members. (To learn more about team-building activities, please read Chapter 13, "Keys to Building a Trustworthy Community" by Cindi Snedaker.)

Evening Retreat Component. In the evenings at Whisper Canyon, youth pastors and adult team leaders minister to students through a retreat program. This includes nightly student-led worship around the campfire followed by a youth pastor or speaker who gives a Bible teaching tailored to eighth- through twelfth-grade students. Youth pastors and small group leaders come alongside and support students throughout the week. (To read about how this outreach trip helps launch students' spiritual journeys, be sure to read Chapter 7, "Launching Spiritual Journeys" by Steve Balsiger.)

3. Adult-led Women's Craft Ministry

In addition to the student-led ministry, a team of adults from PBCC and WGBC meet to organize crafts and Bible teaching for the women of King City. Members of the women's craft team (mostly women and a few men) join us for one or more days as their work schedules allow.

We organize worship music and Bible teachings in Spanish to encourage King City women in their walk with the Lord. Topics vary from year to year and have included PBCC and

WGBC women sharing personal stories of God's work in their lives or facilitating a discussion about a Bible passage. We intentionally choose crafts that foster conversations with the women.

We also offer childcare for babies and young children who are too young to participate in the VBS program. Teens from the VBS program who love working with young children are encouraged to take the lead in supervising these little ones. It's a joy for the women's craft team to work together with students in this way.

Participating in the women's craft ministry year after year allows teens and adults to build lasting relationships with King City women and their families. Having adults and teens serve alongside one another is an easy way to nurture relationships across generations.

The framework of this trip helps usher young people into God's presence and facilitates deep connections between teens and caring adults. While we have not collected scientific data, over the years we've noticed that many students who engaged in PBCC's King City mission trips by making meaningful connections with people and by experiencing God in personal ways are continuing to (1) develop meaningful relationships with peers and adults, (2) serve on mission trips or other ministries, and (3) pursue their relationship with God in college and beyond.

In short, these yearly mission trips help cultivate lasting faith in our youth and adults as God becomes real to them. This is remarkable given the current alarming rate of church dropouts.

As you read these testimonies, I pray you too will be inspired to notice God at work in your own life and to pursue a closer connection with him.

Chapter 3

Signs Point to Jesus

Some of the stories in this book describe visible signs and wonders of God. In the Bible when the Lord performed signs and wonders, they were to demonstrate his supremacy over other gods and creation, to help his followers believe in him, to protect, guide, heal or deliver his people, or to manifest his glory.[16] (See this endnote for a detailed list of Scripture references regarding these signs.)

For those who get excited about signs and wonders (myself included), the cartoon on the next page offers a good reminder:

To help us keep our eyes on the one the signs point to, each testimony is followed by Bible verses to ground us in the gospel message.

II. TESTIMONIES FROM THE VINEYARD

Jesus said, "I am the vine;
you are the branches.
If you remain in me and I in you,
you will bear much fruit."
—John 15:5 NIV

Chapter 4

A Lesson in Faith through Hip-Hop Dance

Shea Charkowsky
Student Team Member, 2015-2018

God surprised me during the King City trip by fulfilling two major goals I had set for myself during my senior year in high school. Because I struggled with social anxiety growing up, my first goal was to become more confident and outgoing. The second was and is my lifelong goal to use the gifts the Lord has given me to bless others.

Pursuing the first goal led me to begin taking hip-hop dance at my school. Soon after I started *Hip-Hop I*, the dance department held auditions for the fall show. I decided to go for it. Since I've always been known for math, robotics, and brain puzzles, people were shocked to see me auditioning. "Whoa!

Shea can dance?!" they said as they watched me perform. I, too, was surprised by how well it went and by how much of a passion hip-hop became for me.

When the King City trip came around, a thought came to mind to teach a dance class at the park with the kids. A few weeks before the trip, even though I hadn't mentioned it out loud, my mom had the same idea. "Hey, Shea, you should totally teach a hip-hop class in King City!"

However, each time I thought about it, I was reluctant. I didn't want to overcommit myself. Schoolwork and an approaching dance show were already taking up a lot of my time, and choreographing a previous dance had taken me weeks to complete. Then again, I also knew teaching the class in King City would fulfill both goals. I was left with a dilemma I chose not to confront, so I kept pushing the decision away.

I forgot about it until Sunday (the day before we began park activities in King City), when Kyle, our high school pastor at the time, gave a convicting evening message. "Think, pray, and ask God, 'Why am I here? Be honest with yourselves," he said. I knew exactly what that question meant for me. In our prayer groups that night, I told my small group there was something God might be calling me to do. I shared that I felt unprepared, but that maybe I just wasn't trusting in him.

The next day, when I started to create a dance, God gave me a sudden new flow of inspiration. The choreography just came to me, and by the time our morning activities were over, I had made a firm decision to start teaching the class the next day. But the decision didn't come from a dramatic leap of faith; it felt more like God's hand was gently lifting me up and leading me into it. He gave me everything I needed, including the faith and confidence to follow through with teaching the class.

In all, about eight students and three adults joined in the class, and three of them learned the whole dance from beginning to end. Seeing people smiling and having fun dancing as I cheered for them made me feel energized and full of joy. On the last night at Whisper Canyon during the annual dance party, two of my peers and I performed the dance while everyone watching whooped and hollered for us.

I was surprised by how much the class enabled me to connect with people, especially those from church whom I likely wouldn't have connected with otherwise. It allowed me to start new conversations with people in the audience because they saw another part of me they hadn't seen before. In addition, the hip-hop class gave me an opportunity to encourage others, something I used to have difficulty with due to social insecurities.

Teaching the class definitely strengthened my faith. I learned that I can be confident in God to complete his plan through me when I'm obedient to his calling. I recognized at a deeper level what it means to be loved and cared for by him. He showed me tangibly how he cares for me even in these small, simple things and that he desires a personal relationship so much that he would provide the faith to make that desire known.

This experience was one of the clearest and most direct steps I've been able to take toward achieving these two goals of becoming more confident and blessing others with my gifts. God gave me the courage to start and lead something despite my uncertainties. He also gave me the confidence to push past my social nervousness, form new relationships, and build others up.

Because of what God did for me in King City, I found myself with increased faith and strengthened trust. Recently while driving to babysit a family friend, I was thinking about what I learned from this trip. I was slightly nervous that I would not be able to keep the kids engaged since one of the two children usually stays in his room when babysitters come. I prayed to

God and thanked him for his gift of faith and for his faithfulness, confident that he would lead the evening. The visit turned out even better than I expected. The three of us spent the entire time together, and at the end of the evening, the boy who usually doesn't interact said our time together was "great fun." Other simple examples like this have helped build my faith and serve as reminders of God's providence.

I'm so grateful for the chance to experience God working through me and in me and to enter into a deeper relationship with him.

Jesus [is] the founder and perfecter
of our faith. —Hebrews 12:2

For by grace you have been saved through faith.
And this is not your own doing; it is the gift of God,
not a result of works, so that no one may boast.
For we are his workmanship,
created in Christ Jesus for good works,
which God prepared beforehand,
that we should walk in them. —Ephesians 2:8-10

As each has received a gift, use it to serve
one another, as good stewards of God's varied grace:
whoever speaks, as one who speaks oracles of God;
whoever serves, as one who serves by the strength
that God supplies—in order that in everything
God may be glorified through Jesus Christ.
To him belong glory and dominion
forever and ever. Amen. —1 Peter 4:10-11

Chapter 5

Amazed by Divine Appointments

Cherie Wolowski
Adult Team Member

As part of the women's ministry team, I trusted God would put me where I needed to be, but I'm still surprised by just how divine my appointments were.

On the first morning of the 2017 trip, I approached a young woman named Shawna, who was holding a newborn baby. She was sitting at one of the classroom tables where we had set up all the materials the ladies would need to make a beaded necklace. I sat down next to her and offered to hold her baby so she could make the craft. As we talked and strung beads together, she began to share the difficulties she was having with breastfeeding. Immediately, I felt God's hand connecting us.

Oh, this is where I'm meant to be!

I've been a lactation consultant for 18 years, so I was able to answer all her questions about breastfeeding. The more we talked, the more she opened up. She said she couldn't afford to pay her own rent, so she lives with her grandparents and her aunt and uncle. They are not supportive of her breastfeeding and do not understand how much she wants to nurse her child. They also criticize her for holding the baby too much, saying she's going to spoil the child. I could see the anguish on her face as she spoke.

I reassured her that she was doing the right things for her baby's development and encouraged her in her efforts. God gave me an opportunity to connect with her each day that week. I explained the reasons why moms can never hold their babies too much. Thankfully her family members were there to hear the information. I knew by this young mom's smiles that she was encouraged and I was blessed in return.

Because of that experience, I had even more faith that God would use me the following year. On the second day of the 2018 mission trip, I was helping with a craft at the park. I randomly sat next to a woman at a picnic table to show her how to sew and decorate a tote bag.

As I was helping Barbara, somehow our conversation got around to her daughter who was having difficulties in school. I could relate to her pain. My now-adult son has dyslexia, which affected his younger years. It turns out that her daughter also needed to be tested for dyslexia.

In that moment, I knew God had strategically placed me there to support her. I shared that although my son found school difficult and continues to struggle with dyslexia, he is managing to keep up and do well in his classes and in his trade of choice. I encouraged her while acknowledging how hard the journey is.

I'm honored to have been able to support her. Barbara and I exchanged cell phone numbers and have remained in touch, both of us blessing each other. When I texted her recently to tell her I was thinking of her, she replied, "So good to get your text, to know you care. I am so blessed to have connected with you. Yesterday in Bible study we talked about God's Spirit and just being there for others. A simple smile, a short greeting. Today you have been that assurance for me."

Such a little thing means so much to both of us.

I have participated in King City's women's ministry since 2016. Each year when I return home, I marvel at how God used me and blessed me during the week. He knows just how to connect people—he sees what's going on in our lives and puts us where we can most benefit somebody else.

LORD, you know everything
there is to know about me.
You perceive every movement
of my heart and soul,
and you understand my every thought
before it even enters my mind. —Psalm 139:1-2 TPT

Blessed be the God and Father of
our Lord Jesus Christ, the Father of mercies
and God of all comfort,
who comforts us in all our affliction,
so that we may be able to comfort those
who are in any affliction,
with the comfort with which we ourselves
are comforted by God. —2 Corinthians 1:3-4

For God chose to save us through our Lord Jesus Christ,
not to pour out his anger on us.
Christ died for us so that, whether we are dead
or alive when he returns,
we can live with him forever.
So encourage each other and build
each other up, just as you are
already doing. —1 Thessalonians 5:9-11 NLT

Chapter 6

Contagious Encounters with God

Thomas Mathen
Student Team Member, 2015-2018

Junior year of high school was the lowest point in my life. So many things were going wrong. It felt like God wasn't there for me and didn't love me. I was so ready to get away for a week at Whisper Canyon and King City. I didn't care that I'd have to work super hard to make up all the classwork I would miss. For now, I was excited to spend time with friends and show love to King City kids again.

I was sitting in the amphitheater at Whisper Canyon during an evening session but had a hard time focusing on the teaching. Problem after problem jumped back and forth in my mind. I'd gotten into a horrible battle with my parents, which made me feel alone and rejected even though I was living with them every day. I hadn't talked to my dad for five months other than throwing out small talk like, "Hey, how's it going?" and not waiting for his answer.

My brother had just left for college and every month that passed made me feel more and more isolated. So I buried myself in school and volleyball but was struggling to get good grades and falling behind in classes. On top of that, I started having pain in my left knee and developed shin splints, which affected my performance as a starting player on the volleyball team and was beginning to destroy my confidence.

Then, in King City when I greeted one of the kids I'd bonded with the year before, he didn't recognize me—another stab to reinforce my feelings of being unloved and alone. I guess I hadn't done enough to create a strong bond with him.

During that evening session, a thought gnawed at me. If God's not with me in the small stuff, he's not going to be with me in the big stuff. Normally, when things go wrong, I put on a happy persona, like everything's okay. But because I was carrying so much with no way of fixing anything, I wasn't able to hide my emotions. After the teaching, the youth pastor dismissed everyone for dessert.

I frowned and stomped up the hill, kicking a pine cone out of my way. Auntie Gabi walked up and asked what was wrong. In India, saying "Auntie" is a sign of respect and endearment to older people you interact with. To me, Auntie Gabi is more than that. She's the mom of one of my best friends, an adult figure I trust to help me in my spiritual walk with God.

As we made our way to the dining area for s'mores, I told her about the boy who forgot who I was, the injuries and adversities I was facing in volleyball, and that I had issues with my parents. She invited me to go for a walk up the gravel road leading into Whisper Canyon to talk. I slowly opened up to her, admitting I didn't know if God was there for me, or if he actually loved me. Immediately, she touched my forearm and stopped me. She prayed, "God, show Tommy he's not alone and that you're here for him."

I lowered my head and closed my eyes.

As we stood there on the dark path in silence, a memory popped up and I saw a golden umbrella over me. God reminded me of something my mom told me years ago. When I was one and a half years old, my parents had a Bible study leader who was a prayer warrior. He asked my mom if she had had any problems during her pregnancy with me. When she said yes, he said, "I see that child under a golden umbrella that God is holding above him. He's always going to be protected and he will always be loved by God."

I had not thought of that memory in years. As I described what God showed me, the heavy weight I'd been feeling lifted. I couldn't believe how God came through and showed himself to me. I smiled ear to ear and felt so much reassurance. In that moment, I knew without a doubt that God had always been watching over me and that he'd always be there for me. He planted the truth about his love deep in my heart.

That night on the gravel road in Whisper Canyon was one of the strongest points in my faith. I had never felt that way before. I can't explain it, but in that moment and since then, I have felt so strong and secure in my faith. When God communicated with me in that personal and tangible way, he solidified my foundation in him and removed a lot of my strong doubts about him being real and being there for me.

He also gave me hope that things would get better. After that encounter with God, I was so willing to forgive my parents, work on the communication problems with them, and forget about the past. When I got home from that trip, I got back on speaking terms with my parents. It's still a work in progress, but being able to talk to my Dad again is a huge improvement to how things were before.

Looking back, I can see now how God has protected me throughout my entire life with things that have happened at school, with my family, and other issues. That experience showed me firsthand that second chances are real. You can think your life is terrible and you could be going through a tough time like nothing is working out your way. But God is always there for you no matter what.

And the amazing thing is, God did something even bigger that not only affected me but another entire family.

The following year in King City, I hit it off right away with a four-year-old boy named Miguelito. We had so much fun jumping and dancing together during the VBS songs. He climbed up on my back and I carried him around on my shoulders. Then later when he saw me play the part of Jesus in the Bible story skit, he jumped up and started cheering, "TOMMY! TOMMY!" I broke character for a second and glanced over at him with a smile.

That same year, Jordan, one of my best friends, made a connection with Miguelito's older brother, Rubén. The four of us had a great time hanging out together. On the last day of VBS when we said our good-byes, I was already missing Miguelito. Because I was graduating from high school, I didn't think I'd be able to see him again. Although I'd be going to college nearby, I doubted I'd be able to go on the mission trip the following year because missing college classes and making up course work would be much harder.

Miguelito was only four years old at the time, so he didn't seem to be affected much when we left. I thought about him a lot after that trip and put a picture of him on the back of my phone. Looking at it made me smile and reminded me of all the good times we had. As it got close to the King City trip the following year, I wondered, *Is it even possible for me to go? Even for a day or two? And is it worth it?* Then I thought, *What's more important? School or serving in King City?*

When I heard that Jordan and another one of my best friends were going on the trip, I suddenly got motivated to make it happen. I talked to my professors and worked it out so I could be at VBS for two days. I had no idea if Miguelito would be there because some of the kids don't come to our VBS program every year. So when I spotted him across the room with his brother, I yelled out, "MIGUELITO! What's up?"

His eyes lit up, he ran over to me, and I gave him a big hug. Seeing him brought back so many fun memories from the previous year. We had a ton of fun that day playing soccer, basketball, and getting our faces painted. At the end of the week, Miguelito gave me a card thanking me for missing school and coming to hang out with him. It meant the world to know how much he appreciated my being there.

Weeks later, I heard something that amazed me.

Miguelito's mom, Veronica, told one of our adult team members that after the VBS when I first met Miguelito, he told his mom, "I want to do the same things Tommy does. I want to go to church and sing the songs I learned with my friends Tommy and Jordan." Veronica said her boys became closer to God and are growing in the Lord because of how Jordan and I loved God.

I was shocked to hear this. Miguelito got his entire family to go to church, and he was only four years old at the time. Soon after that, Veronica and her husband also started going to Bible study. I couldn't believe what God had done just by me and Jordan playing with Miguelito and Rubén and showing them love.

I never thought my interactions could have that big of an effect on anyone. Through this experience, God showed me I'm capable of serving him well and that I have an impact on people's lives. It made me feel more confident in working with kids and motivated me to work at a local Christian camp serving sixth through twelfth graders. I've been able to speak into kids' lives. I love just hanging out with them and building trust with them by sharing my own experiences and struggles of how God has helped me through them. I love encouraging them that no matter what they are going through, God is there with them, always.

I won't ever forget how God spoke to me that night on the path during my junior year in high school. He made himself real to me during the worst year of my life. And a year later, God made himself real to Miguelito's entire family and now he's working in their lives, too.

Experiencing God's love through my relationship with Miguelito has brought me even closer to God because he showed me how much he loves us, and how he calls us to show that love to one another. That makes me want to pursue God even more.

I love the LORD, because he has heard
my voice and my pleas for mercy.
Because he inclined his ear to me,
therefore I will call on him
as long as I live. —Psalm 116:1-2

When you demonstrate the same love
I [Jesus] have for you by loving one another,
everyone will know that you're
my true followers. —John 13:35 TPT

I [Jesus] am the sprouting vine, you are the branches.
As you live in union with me
as your source, fruitfulness will
stream from within you. —John 15:5 TPT

Chapter 7

Launching Spiritual Journeys

Steve Balsiger
PBCC Boys' Small Group Leader since 2005

King City has been more than just a service trip. It's been a way for me to deepen the relationship I have with our students. From my perspective as a small group leader, I've been struck by the transformational experience it provides to our PBCC/WGBC students. When I meet up with students who graduated years ago and we reflect on their time in high school, the thing we talk about most often is their experience on the King City outreach trips.

But often instead of talking about the impact *they* had on a child's life, students talk about the impact the trip had on their *own* lives. Spiritual journeys are launched, shaped, and grown on this trip. For some, the King City trip provides a spiritual atmosphere and supportive community for them to consider a relationship with Christ for the first time. Whether they have been attending church for many years or they were unchurched and invited to King City by a friend, the trip opens the doors of their hearts, allowing them to think deeply about their relationship with the Lord. I think the combination of time away from their busy, stress-filled lives, the immersion into an intentionally loving community, and serving those in need all contribute to softening one's heart towards God.

The trip often changes the spiritual direction of a student's life not just through the ministry but also through the prep meetings, sharing of stories, time at Whisper Canyon, and the community they share with the team. Because of the trust that is built amongst our youth group community, students feel comfortable sharing their testimonies of how God has been working in their lives, where they are in their faith, or what they're struggling with. When students share deep, painful, and personal life experiences in a group, they expose their heart to team members, allowing us to know them better.

It also gives those listening opportunities to encourage them, give them advice, speak truth into their pain, and let them know they're not alone. For those students who have already experienced healing from God or sensed God in their pain, we rejoice and celebrate with them, praising God for his wonderful work in their lives. Hearing about their victories brings us all closer to the Lord, and helps us realize he will be there for us, too, should we experience something similar in the future. The whole process strengthens faith in those sharing and those listening to the testimonies.

Years after their last trip, many students I've talked to have shared that King City was a turning point in their faith. I don't think it's going too far to say that this service trip is probably the most significant event of each school year for our students.

But whenever someone turns to the Lord,
the veil is taken away.
For the Lord is the Spirit, and wherever
the Spirit of the Lord is, there is freedom.
So all of us who have had that veil removed
can see and reflect the glory of the Lord.
And the Lord—who is the Spirit—makes us
more and more like him as we are changed
into his glorious image. —2 Corinthians 3:16-18 NLT

So faith comes from hearing,
and hearing through
the word of Christ. —Romans 10:17

Jesus replied, "I tell you for certain that you
must be born from above before you
can see God's kingdom!" —John 3:3 CEV

To learn more about how to support students when they return from mission trips or spiritual retreats, be sure to read Chapter 24, "Preparing for Re-entry: Simple Strategies that Work."

Chapter 8

My Faith Ignited

Hannah Camp
Student Team Member, 2018, 2019

Before going to King City in 2018, my freshman year, I wasn't seeing God move in my life and I didn't care about getting to know him. But watching how he tangibly moved in little Brittany's life was honestly the most jaw-dropping thing I have ever observed; it completely transformed my relationship with him.

On the second day of VBS, I was sitting with Francesca, a King City mom I'd connected with the previous year and whose kids I'd taken care of the day before. We were in the nursery with her baby and her four-year-old, Brittany, during free time. She looked discouraged and told me Brittany never learns in Sunday school because she can't understand or speak any English and has a hard time focusing. I noticed Brittany would always run to the door and go outside instead of sitting and listening. Somebody would always have to chase her and bring her back.

Watching Francesca's disappointment made my heart drop. I wanted to help them, but didn't know how, so I prayed, *God, please help them.*

The next day, I sat down with Francesca again and she looked a lot different, a lot happier. Instead of looking exhausted, I could see joy on her face and I wondered why she was so happy. Francesca said when Brittany got home from camp the day before, she recited the VBS story with very clear details. My teammates had presented a skit of Jesus inviting Peter to walk out on the water, Peter becoming afraid and sinking, and Jesus pulling him out.

"I couldn't even believe what she was telling me!" Francesca said.

"What do you mean?" I asked. "Did someone translate it for her?"

"No. There wasn't anyone else who could do that."

I could barely speak. How is that even possible?

She explained how Brittany completely understood the lesson we taught even without comprehending any English. I don't know how Brittany heard one word of it because it didn't look like she was paying attention during the skit and she couldn't sit still.

Francesca was also amazed. "It's crazy how God can work in people."

This was the first time I had witnessed God intervene in a child's life. He helped her pay attention and translated the Bible story from English to Spanish to help her understand it. Brittany's behavior also seemed more controlled. She looked calmer the rest of the week, not as jittery as I'd seen her the day before. All of this was so astonishing to me. Not only was this experience moving for Francesca and Brittany, but when I shared this story later that night in the large group at Whisper Canyon, I realized God did this for *my* benefit as well.

Before this trip, I wasn't feeling close to the Lord. I didn't talk to him and church wasn't important to me. I'd plan sleepovers on Saturday nights so I wouldn't have to go to church because I didn't have any friends there. I also felt like he wasn't hearing my prayers and didn't listen to me when I talked to him.

But seeing the Lord work alongside Francesca and Brittany completely changed my mindset about him. I now know that God is real, and that he can do anything.

After I got back from King City, instead of feeling distant from God, I felt closer to him and I knew I wasn't alone. I know he's holding me and he's there for me. I feel noticed and acknowledged by him, and that gives me comfort. Even though I didn't have close friends at church, I started going regularly. I was okay being part of the youth group because I knew God was with me. I'm now reading stories about God, I joined a faith club at school, and I ask my friends how I can pray for them. I talk to God all the time: when I'm home, when I'm about to perform for cheer, or wherever I am. God is my friend. I don't have to only talk to him at night. I can talk to him anytime, and I know he's always there.

This experience at King City and the other stories I heard from this trip gave me hope and showed me real life examples of how the Lord can work in us. The trip itself motivated me to attend a week-long Christian camp a few months later, which is where I created all the friendships I have with church friends today. It also made me realize I want to make service projects and retreats a regular part of my life. Although it takes up my spring break, I'm looking forward to going back to King City every year while I'm in high school.

Jesus said, "These things I have spoken
to you while I am still with you.
But the Helper, the Holy Spirit,
whom the Father will send
in my name, he will teach you all things
and bring to your remembrance
all that I have said to you." —John 14:25-26

Though the LORD is on high,
Yet He regards the lowly;
But the proud He knows
from afar. —Psalm 138:6, NKJV

If God is for us, who can be against us?
He who did not spare his own Son
but gave him up for us all,
how will he not also with him
graciously give us
all things? —Romans 8:31b-32

Chapter 9

Pruned into Fatherhood

Brian Watson
Adult Team Leader

On my first trip to King City, I parked the minivan full of PBCC high school students at Saint John's Catholic Church for our first day of VBS. I walked into the church for a moment but felt so out of place that I retreated to the van to hide. *What am I here for?*

My mind was still wrapped up in my work, addicted to my phone and email inbox. I struggled to disconnect from my professional life, which made it difficult to serve the King City youth. I was in my first year as the director of a fast-paced non-profit organization, working intense hours and trying to impress the senior management. Three days before this trip, we had just completed our marquee fundraiser, which raises 45% of our budget. I would arrive late to the King City training meetings still thinking about work, then leave immediately when they ended. Because of this, I had not formed connections with our PBCC students.

Ryan Hinn, youth pastor at the time, noticed me sitting inside the van alone. Ryan had given my wife and me pre-marriage counseling and performed our ceremony. He walked up to me and said, "Watson, some of the kids in there are growing up without fathers and don't have adult role models that spend time with them. The kids just need you to play with them." He also reminded me how badly I needed this trip and motivated me to go inside.

I began by helping corral loose baseballs and by talking to the kids who were waiting in line to bat. Throughout the week, I gradually began to feel more comfortable interacting with the kids. I noticed one of the boys hitting the ball really hard, so I encouraged him by telling him he was the best home run slugger in King City. Another day when I saw a boy kicking a soccer ball by himself, I went over and kicked it around with him. As we played together, I encouraged him to join a team. I then learned the home run slugger was his cousin. I eventually developed a friendship with these two boys and another cousin, all fifth-grade boys.

The three cousins and I sat together during craft time at the end of the morning. I was clueless about how to assemble the crafts but it didn't matter. Together, the boys and I found a way to put them together and they went home feeling great about what they created.

As an extension of the VBS program, follow-up questions were written on index cards and given to PBCC/WGBC students and adults. We used the questions to help King City kids connect with Jesus through the Bible stories we had presented in the morning. Later at the park, I paired up with one or two PBCC students and called over a few King City kids. I enjoyed facilitating this interaction and talking to the kids about Jesus. By the end of the trip, I realized this is where God wanted me to be and that he could use me. I did belong here.

Returning to King City for a second year, I focused on the baseball ministry both in the mornings at Saint John's and at the park in the afternoons. Teaching kids the fundamentals gave me purpose. I taught them how to field a ground ball, how to hit a line drive, how to run the bases well, and how to throw a ball. I enjoyed being their biggest cheerleader, high-fiving them, and offering encouragement when I saw them make good contact with the ball or have good speed on the base path. I gave them relentless praise and they got fired up hearing their name called out.

I developed my strongest connections to the King City youth on the baseball field, and I cherish those interactions. I think about their smiles, their laughter, their expressions of joy when it was their turn to bat, and when they accomplished a skill for the very first time that surprised even them.

One child ran up to me saying, "Hey, Coach Brian, I'm gonna show up tomorrow and give 110% of what I've got!" The joy on his face made my day.

Another child who played baseball all three days said, "Hey Coach Brian, I don't know if I'm gonna play baseball tomorrow."

"Eddie, that's fine, buddy." I said to him. "What is it you want to do?"

He tilted his head back, thought really hard, then said, "I think I wanna go fly a kite."

I think about that often and would love to be Eddie, where my most difficult decision is whether to play baseball or fly a kite! I desire that same simplicity, and love seeing the world through Eddie's eyes. Images of these kids remain in my mind and heart throughout the year, and I can honestly say a week of King City baseball enriched my life.

When I returned for my third year on this ministry trip, my wife, Kaela, was 36 weeks pregnant. She had joined me on the trip the previous two years, but stayed home because of the baby. Despite this perfect excuse not to go on the trip, my heart was so ready to fully enter in this time. I was now familiar with the trip, knew what to expect, and felt more connected with our PBCC high school community because I had attended the training meetings.

I was also excited because three boys from the weekly small group I co-led had finally decided to come. My small group's attendance on the King City trip had been dismal in past years, so I had been praying for them to join us. I was looking forward to connecting with them more deeply and making an impact on the kids in King City. Thankfully, Kaela granted me permission to go.

On the first day of our VBS program, I immediately reconnected with King City kids from the previous years. I enjoyed helping with the baseball ministry again and looked forward to spending the entire week bonding with them.

But that evening during dinner at Whisper Canyon, I received a scary phone call from my wife. She said that during a routine check-up that day, doctors noticed irregular blood flow through the umbilical cord. They were concerned our baby was not receiving adequate nutrition and were considering inducing my wife the next day, depending on more test results.

I will never forget Kaela's words on that phone call. "Brian, you need to come home. The baby is coming!"

The urgency in her voice told me she was shaken and that this was serious. Students and adult leaders began praying for my wife and baby.

The next morning, I went into town for the second day of VBS with my luggage packed. My trip had come to an end early. I would be getting a ride home with Ryan because all of the other vehicles were needed to transport our students from Whisper Canyon to King City and back.

When it came time to leave St. John's in the morning, I was hit with a whirlwind of emotions. I wasn't ready to say goodbye to King City. My eyes filled with tears as I thought of leaving the kids. I was also disappointed I wouldn't get to bond with the boys from my PBCC small group, whom I had prayed for. I really wanted to finish the trip. But I also had an amazing life event awaiting me; the birth of my first-born child. When I received goodbye hugs from adult leaders Cindi, Stevo, and Eli, it hit me.

My trip is over. But when I leave, I'm going to go be a dad!

I walked out of Saint John's, jumped into Ryan's vehicle, and away we went to my wife's doctor's appointment. That evening, back at Whisper Canyon, when students and adult leaders broke into prayer groups, they continued praying for my wife and baby. They told me later that they had asked God to keep our daughter safe, that she would receive the necessary oxygen, that all the nutrition she needed would flow freely through the umbilical cord, and that Kaela would be safe, healthy, and at peace.

God answered those Whisper Canyon prayers. The results came back fine. Doctors confirmed our baby was healthy and all was well. They felt comfortable allowing my wife's pregnancy to continue, and Kaela allowed me to return to King City. I'm so thankful God kept my wife and baby safe, and allowed me to finish out the week.

When I look back at that first year, I realize that if I had never stepped out of the van, I wouldn't have experienced what God had in store for me. Although I had felt inadequate, I quickly learned I could use my gifts and love of sports to serve the kids of King City. God pulled me out of a shallow, self-centered world where my priorities were focused on work, and showed me there's more I could do that would have an eternal impact. God used the trip as an important disruption to center me. For one week out of the year, I now know I'm called to serve and be present with kids in King City, helping them develop their relationship with Jesus. God has used this trip to help me reduce the tension between my personal and professional life. Working towards a healthier work-life balance helps expand my capacity for relationships with my wife, child, church family at PBCC, and beyond. It's through those connections that I am learning to experience the open, loving heart of my heavenly Father.

If anyone serves me, he must follow me;
and where I am, there will my servant be also.
If anyone serves me,
the Father will honor him. —John 12:26

Do not be conformed to this world,
but be transformed
by the renewal of your mind,
that by testing you may discern
what is the will of God,
what is good and acceptable
and perfect. —Romans 12:2

I have been crucified with Christ.
It is no longer I who live,
but Christ who lives in me.
And the life I now live in the flesh
I live by faith in the Son of God,
who loved me
and gave himself for me. —Galatians 2:20

Chapter 10

Breaking Out of Me-Culture to Love God & Love People

George Mathen
Student Team Member, 2013-2015
Student Team Leader, 2016

As a starting freshman on the varsity volleyball team in 2013, I placed a high value on sports. I didn't want to go on the King City trip because I'd have to miss a whole week of practice and two games. I knew if I went, the coach would penalize me by benching me when I returned. I was very independent-minded, constantly focusing on how to better myself and how to prepare myself for my future career.

However, my mom nudged me into the trip, saying in the grand scheme of things it would be more important for me to go. So I went.

It was in King City where I first met Paco, a second-grader at the time, his two little sisters, and five older cousins. Because there were so many kids living in one house, Paco absolutely loved it when I would carry him on my shoulders because he received focused attention for a change.

When I got back from King City, sure enough, I was benched for most of the game, which made me feel frustrated and eager to play. However, I was beginning to see the value our ministry team provided to the King City kids. We gave them hope that there was something better than what they were going through and someone greater to cling to (i.e. God) in moments of despair. The impact the ministry had on the people of King City was invaluable, and I explained this to my coach.

As a sophomore, I knew going on the trip would not only mean risking my spot as the starting setter, but it would also negatively affect our season because as the starting setter, I played a key role in the team's success. I went anyway because my time in King City had moved my heart so deeply. The benefits of loving on underprivileged children and giving them hope in God far outweighed the consequences of missing two volleyball games. To my surprise, Coach did not bench me when I returned.

Junior year, I remember saying, "Okay God, I'm going to give this volleyball week up to you." I had no hesitation missing games because I knew what I was doing for the Lord was far more important than playing volleyball.

That year when I saw Paco again, my eyes lit up. We raced to each other and I picked him up and spun him around. We grew closer to each other, which made it harder to say goodbye at the end of the week. We dreamed about running off as best pals and hanging out for the rest of our lives. But when I looked into his eyes, I realized that he actually wasn't joking. So I told him, "Here's what we can do: Let's make sure we come back next year and spend every moment of the week together." We now had something to look forward to and I left inspired to come back. I wanted to leave something for Paco and the other children to hold onto for the rest of their lives.

As a team leader during my senior year, I was allowed to look through the donation boxes for one item that represented the pink color team I was in charge of. I found a pink baseball cap and wore it throughout the week.

As promised, Paco and I met up again for the week and we picked up right where we left off. We spent quality time together laughing, playing four-square, and just being happy together. And at the end of it all, as a parting gift, I gave Paco a bracelet that I commissioned a friend to make. It was crafted of rope and had an anchor and wooden beads that spelled "HOPE" on it. I chose the word hope because these kids needed something to hold onto when facing tough times. As I wrapped it around his wrist, I looked into his eyes and said, "No matter what happens, remember, God is always with you. He will never leave you nor forsake you. It's this truth that will help you move forward."

On my final night in Whisper Canyon, while my friends and I were sitting around the campfire sharing God-moments from the week, we discovered the heart of what this mission trip is all about. I was wearing my pink baseball cap, the one tangible item that represents the culmination of my four trips to King City. That conversation was so impactful that even now as a student at Westmont College, I still speak about it to this day. We were talking about spiritual highs, the increased desire to pursue God fervently during and after a mission trip or retreat—why they happen and why that strong desire tends to fade when we go home. There were many opinions, but one thought resonated with me.

Oftentimes, we get caught up in our busy lives of the Bay Area. The priority is ourselves and our future. What can I do to further my resume? What can I do for myself? Because of that individualistic focus, we often fail to notice those around us. On the other hand, when on a mission trip or retreat, the priority becomes looking out for one another and simply loving each other. As a result, our whole perspective shifts and we are now looking through a new relational lens where everyone is "on fire for God." This shift in focus encourages us to love God and show that same love to those around us. To put it simply, love God and love people.

Throughout the years, God was working in my coach, too—he never benched me after my freshman year for missing a week of practice. In fact, before my senior year season, the coach even tried to reschedule the games around the King City trip! This was astonishing because coaches rarely did such a thing. In the end, we had successful seasons, becoming league champions and advancing to the playoffs for the first time in program history. I still chuckle in amazement at how God blessed my decision to pursue his work instead of my own. Ultimately, God's plans for me were far bigger and better than what I could ever imagine for myself and I cherish this truth.

It was on this senior year trip that I realized the need to let go of my individualistic culture and instead internalize the message, "Love God. Love people." It has taught me to be more balanced, more relationally oriented than task-oriented, and to look to God to work in my heart and in the relationships I engage in. Now, when a friend needs to talk, I'll often drop what I'm doing and speak with them; rather than being on my cell phone during meal times, I now make it a point to nurture relationships.

And everywhere I go, I still carry my pink baseball cap, either wearing it or hanging it off my backpack. The pink hat is a reminder for me of my time in King City and what God has done in the hearts of the people and what he *can* do. It's a reminder amidst my busyness to not fall back to the old ways but to surrender my agenda to God and remain intentional with those around me.

"Teacher, which is the great commandment
in the Law?" And [Jesus] said to him,
"You shall love the Lord your God with all your heart
and with all your soul and with all your mind.
This is the great and first commandment.
And a second is like it:
You shall love your neighbor as yourself.
On these two commandments depend all the Law
and the Prophets." —Matthew 22:36-40

With one sacrifice
Christ made his people
perfect forever. They are the ones who are
being made holy. The Holy Spirit also tells us
about this. First he says, "This is the agreement
I will make with my people in the future,"
says the Lord. "I will put my laws in their hearts.
I will write my laws
in their minds." —Hebrews 10:14-16 ERV

It is to your advantage that I [Jesus] go away,
for if I do not go away, the Helper will not come to you.
But if I go, I will send him to you....
When the Spirit of truth comes,
he will guide you into all the truth,
for he will not speak on his own authority,
but whatever he hears he will speak,
and he will declare to you
the things that are to come. —John 16:7, 13

Chapter 11

Being a Father to the Fatherless

Jano Banks
Adult Team Member

King City 2018 was the first mission trip I'd ever been on. My wife and three kids had gone multiple times and raved about their experiences. But I wasn't sure how I, a 52-year-old dad, would relate to a bunch of kids on an outreach program. I simply didn't know what to expect.

When we arrived at St. John's Catholic Church, I immediately saw our high school students connecting with King City kids. Teens who had been on past trips were finding kids they already knew and exchanging hugs and smiles. I was thinking it would be great to connect with someone from King City, but I wasn't sure I'd have the opportunity.

I figured I'd serve the kids by helping George Stoyko, the adult in charge of the baseball ministry. George has ministered on this trip since the year 2000, first in Mexicali, and then in King City beginning in 2008. He brings a truckload of baseball equipment, including a portable batting cage, a bucketful of wiffle balls, and some plastic bats.

As soon as he started setting up the net on the blacktop, kids of all sizes lined up to hit soft-toss pitches from George and others on his team. Having coached my own children in Little League, I took over for George after a while so he could hang out with kids and help them bat. He seemed to enjoy the break from pitching because, for the rest of the week, I threw soft toss after soft toss; I must have thrown over 500 soft toss pitches that week!

On the first day, a group of girls came by to hit wiffle balls. When I took a break from pitching, they asked if I would play catch with them. It was a simple game—throw and catch a wiffle ball. We enhanced it by counting how many times in a row we could catch the ball without dropping it. After about a half-hour, I had to go back to my soft toss pitching duty. It was nice to play catch with the girls, but it didn't strike me as anything special.

On one of the days, George was a bit late in bringing the baseball equipment to the St. John's playground. At the start of the day, Alicia, a fourth-grader who had played catch with me the day before, came right up to me and asked to play catch again. Since there were no wiffle balls yet, we had to improvise. We played catch with a big rubber ball. When George arrived, I needed to help him set up the soft toss, ending the game of catch with Alicia.

On the last day when George was late again, Alicia came outside, greeted me with a hug, and asked me to play catch. During worship time that day, she stood next to me so we could sing together. We then sat at the same circle group for the craft, which involved decorating a red paper heart and lacing yarn around the edges. Since it was the last day, she gave me her craft as a parting gift. When I looked at it, I saw that she had written, "To: Jano, From: Alicia" on the back with a purple marker. I was really touched and wanted to give her something in return. I remembered seeing some of our students giving their name buttons to King City kids, so I gave her my name button.

As we sat there side-by-side, I kept wondering why this one girl had wanted to hang out with me. I soon found out when I asked about her family. Alicia pointed out her older brother who was also at the VBS. She then showed me a picture on her phone of the two of them standing next to a memorial to her father who had died when she was a baby.

Alicia was seeking a father figure, and I fit the bill.

During the prep meetings before the trip, I asked for prayer because I was worried I wouldn't make a connection with anyone. I could never have guessed this was how God would use me. I threw all those soft tosses to serve the kids, almost like a robotic pitcher. I was treating it like a job, doing my duty as an outreach program volunteer. But it was in the simple games of catch where God did his work through me and caught my heart.

When Alicia asked me to play with her, I could tell she genuinely wanted to be close to me and spend time with me. Her personal attention made me feel loved by a daughter, something I never expected to happen on this trip.

In the end, I added more value than I ever thought I could. And in return, I received something totally unexpected—the heart-felt love from a little girl who allowed me to temporarily substitute for her dad. It was such an honor to be able to fill his shoes for a few days.

However, God is the only one who can ultimately fill her dad's shoes. What a comfort to know that Alicia has a heavenly Father who loves her unconditionally and will never leave her nor forsake her. She is his beloved daughter, fully accepted and perfectly loved.

Be strong and courageous.
Do not be afraid or terrified because
of them, for the LORD your God
goes with you; he will never leave you
nor forsake you. —Deuteronomy 31:6 NIV

For all who are led by the Spirit of God
are children of God. So you have not received
a spirit that makes you fearful slaves.
Instead, you received God's Spirit
when he adopted you as his own children.
Now we call him,
"Abba, Father." —Romans 8:14-15 NLT

And behold, I [Jesus] am with you always,
to the end of the age. —Matthew 28:20

Chapter 12

Noticing the Presence of God

Esther Need
Student Team Member, 2015-2018

My weeks in King City were special times. Precious times. Times when I sensed the presence of God. It didn't matter where I was, whether at Whisper Canyon, the church site, or the park, God was clearly present.

I saw him in the laughter, the smiles of tired friends, and the hands sticky from crafts. The very air seemed to testify of God. I often wondered what made those giggles and messes different from the ones at home? God is always with me. Yet I am not aware of him at home like I am on the King City trips.

As I look back on my four years of high school, life was crazy. Wake up. Go to school. Do homework. Play sports. Hang out with friends. Do more homework. Remember to sleep. Repeat.

Despite how fast a day went by, I carved out a little time for the Lord each morning. Matthew 7:7 says, "Ask and it will be given to you; seek and you will find; knock and the door will be opened to you." I longed to seek God, to knock, and for him to reveal himself to me. But my little time with God was simply little. It never impacted my other interactions; lunch, sports, and homework were not done with him in mind.

The mission trips to King City were different. God infiltrated all the moments of our days. We went there simply to serve, to seek God, and to show the love of Christ to others. That's all we did. Without the pressure of homework and the busyness of life, I became more aware of him.

I sensed God every moment while I served. When I'd wake up with my friends at 5:30 a.m. to scramble eggs,[17] I was doing it to bring the joy of full tummies to my fellow servants and I knew he was there. During VBS at the church site, I felt his presence as I was serving and loving the children, which sometimes meant leading the craft for that day. Other times it meant playing duck-duck-goose with only two kids who wanted to play, while the rest of the children were absorbed with other activities.

In the afternoon at the park, my expression of love was painting the kids' faces and letting them scribble paint on mine. My terrible versions of Spider-Man or butterflies made the children's faces light up. All of these things reminded me of God's presence.

I also sensed him when we worshiped. In the evenings at Whisper Canyon, we praised him together as one body in his living temple of creation that surrounded us. Our voices sounded out, imperfect but whole, and the quiet night accompanied us as the hills also lifted their praise to the Creator God. For a moment, we joined with nature and reflected the perfection of God out of the broken creation that we are. Despite the day's exhaustion, this body still had a willingness to seek God.

Serving in King City gave me a taste of a life fully lived in the presence of God. We drove down as a group of students and adults to do his work, and somewhere along the line, this body of Christ knocked and God opened the door. Every moment, we were surrounded by God and everything we did reminded us that he was right there with us. We never took our eyes off of him. There was an expectation that God would tangibly reveal himself to us. And he did.

In my walk with God, there's been a gradual shift in how I see him. I now realize that each moment in my life is service to him. It doesn't matter if I'm talking to my best friend or working with someone I've never met. How I treat them is an act of service. My relationship with God is no longer just a little moment in the morning, it's every moment I share with someone else. He is always present with me and he cares about every action I take. He always has. Now I'm beginning to take time to notice.

We love because God first
loved us. —1 John 4:19

'Lord, when did we see you hungry
and feed you,
or thirsty and give you drink?
And when did we see you
a stranger and welcome you,
or naked and clothe you?'
And the King will answer them,
'Truly, I say to you, as you did it to
one of the least of these my brothers,
you did it to me.' —Matthew 25:37-40

But if we walk in the light, as he is in the light,
we have fellowship with one another,
and the blood of Jesus his Son
cleanses us from all sin. —1 John 1:7

Chapter 13

Keys to Building a Trustworthy Community

Cindi Snedaker
PBCC Girls' Small Group Leader, 2000-2018

In addition to serving the families of King City, an equally important aspect of this trip is how we intentionally disciple our eighth- through twelfth-grade students. Two of the ways youth pastors and adult leaders care for them are through the sharing of personal stories before the trip and through opportunities during the trip to affirm individuals for who they are and how God has gifted them. These opportunities include notes of encouragement, specific times of prayer for individuals, and affirmations. Although these activities focus on individual students, they are also powerful team-building exercises.

Testimonies

Every year as part of our month-long training for this ministry trip, we ask students to write a testimony describing where they are on their journey with God and how he is working in their lives. It is a process that helps them reflect on significant moments, relationships, and experiences that have shaped them. During the VBS prep meetings, we set aside time to give every student, and as many adults as time allows, a chance to share their story with the rest of the team.

Since our desire is to get to know one another more deeply and become unified as a team, we encourage them to be as vulnerable as they can with the group. The more authentic we are with each other, the more connected we become. For most students and adults, there is some amount of fear connected to this experience. Most people who share their testimony for the first time worry that exposing their failures or weaknesses may result in judgment or some form of rejection from those who listen. Because we recognize these and other risks, we follow each testimony with words of care and a time of prayer, often physically gathering around a student who has expressed deeper hurts or needs. We are intentional about trying to create a safe environment for students to trust us and each other with their personal struggles, and we reinforce the need for the entire team to keep what is shared private and confidential.

As a result, some students have had the freedom to share things they may never have told anyone else. We also emphasize that every student is at a different place in their journey and that no story is insignificant. The sharing ends up ranging from homework stress or challenges in friendships to deeper issues such as struggles with depression, anxiety, rejection, pornography, identity issues, or grief over a deceased loved one. We encourage students to recognize and share ways they have experienced God and have seen his hand at work in their lives.

Although some of these students may appear to have it all together, it is always profoundly moving to witness their vulnerability as they reveal both good and hard events that have shaped them.

Once they risk sharing their story and find they are met with grace and acceptance, something beautiful happens. There is a possibility for freedom and healing when hidden parts of their lives are exposed, brought into the light, and received with kindness, love, compassion, and prayer. Heavy burdens are often lifted off their shoulders, and many of them experience the power of prayer. When God enters those moments, it is profound; they experience in a tangible way how Jesus receives them with unconditional love and acceptance because of how we, as his family, have received them. We care deeply about these teenagers and it is an honor and privilege to hear their stories.

And as they update their testimonies year after year, they begin to see a bit more of the bigger story God is writing in their lives. This process causes them to notice and remember other times they have experienced him and to acknowledge what they are lacking or desiring with him. Hearing about other people's journeys and reflecting on and sharing their testimonies resets their focus on God and prepares them to be open to experience him on the trip. Those who are seeking more of him begin to recognize when he's moving and working in and through their lives.

This process of opening up the deeper parts of ourselves with one another helps unite and bond the team more than anything else we do. Students feel more connected to each other when they hear how someone else has experienced something similar to what they have gone through, and it helps give greater compassion for those they might not have understood or connected with before.

Affirmations

In addition to affirming students after they share their testimonies, we provide three other opportunities for them to be affirmed by each other while we are in King City. These include writing "Barnabas notes" of encouragement to each other, praying for and sending off our high school seniors at the end of the week, and affirming one another in a circle of affirmation. These activities help put closure on the week of ministry together.

Barnabas Notes. Our notes of encouragement to each other have been named after Barnabas, a follower of Jesus, who was known for being an encourager. During our time at Whisper Canyon, adults and students write Barnabas notes to affirm each other and leave them on the Barnabas bulletin board for that individual to find. Those who receive a note are asked to write notes to two other people to keep the momentum going throughout the week. Students and adults alike look forward to giving and receiving these. During the demanding week of ministry, they provide a boost to help spur each other on and become something tangible they can bring home with them to look back on and remember after the trip is over.

Senior Send-Off. When our week of ministry has concluded, we reserve Friday for a day of reflection and closure together. After a large-group time of open sharing of how we have seen God show up throughout the week, we take the time to pray for our high school seniors in particular. The seniors stand as students and adults gather around them to pray for them, express gratitude for the impact they have made, and commission them for all that lies ahead. This becomes a powerful experience for them of being sent off to continue living for Jesus wherever God takes them. We end this time by receiving communion together, remembering Jesus' sacrifice for us.

Affirmation Circles. Our most powerful opportunity to encourage each other occurs after communion at the very end of the week. We gather with our team in a circle of affirmation where each person, one at a time, is acknowledged, affirmed and encouraged by other students and adults in the group. We take three to five minutes for each person, recognizing how we see God in them or saying something we have appreciated about them, something positive we saw them do during the week of ministry, something about their character, their spiritual gifts, or how they have blessed others. Often, the testimonies that were shared leading up to the trip are woven into these affirmations and celebrated. These moments become beautiful opportunities to see God work in the midst of, and often through, a person's brokenness, fears, or weaknesses, bringing glory to him and highlighting how much he loves us.

Affirmation circles allow students and adults to be seen individually and recognized for their gifting. Many times they are acknowledged for positive or unique qualities they were not aware of or had never heard before. As we share, we are calling each other the name of our becoming: the person God created us to be. There is something very powerful about hearing positive words spoken over you in front of a large group of people. As each person receives these affirmations without speaking, there is often healing that takes place, especially for those who struggle with self-esteem or identity issues. For those who struggle with depression, anxiety, or rejection, hearing the truth about who they are in Christ helps to counteract the lies they have believed about themselves.

This experience also changes how we look at one another. The process of having to identify only the positive and speaking only words that are uplifting and encouraging helps each of us look at each other through a lens of grace. Spending several minutes on each person, culminating into several hours together as a team, gives each person a chance to hear from more than just one team member and allows for others to hear things they had not previously known about that person and their impact on others.

After a week of pouring out love and compassion to the kids of King City, this exercise is profoundly moving for students and adults alike. It leaves a deep and lasting impression on everyone who walks away from it because it highlights what God has done in and through individuals while also expanding our understanding of what happened on the trip. When we hear someone being affirmed, we know so much more about how God moved that week. We all walk away with a greater picture of the powerful ways God worked among us.

The circles of affirmation create a beautiful bookend to the testimonies that were shared at the beginning of the trip. Students and adults have risked vulnerability at the beginning, and then are affirmed at the end, allowing them the opportunity to feel known, loved, and accepted. We leave feeling more centered in the Lord, and with a deeper appreciation of our brothers and sisters in Christ.

You will bring God glory
when you accept and welcome one another
as partners, just at the Anointed One
has fully accepted you and received you
as his partner. —Romans 15:7 TPT

There is therefore now no condemnation
for those who are in Christ Jesus.
For the law of the Spirit of life
has set you free in Christ Jesus
from the law of sin and death. —Romans 8:1

Therefore, if anyone is in Christ,
he is a new creation.
The old has passed away;
behold, the new has come. —2 Corinthians 5:17

Chapter 14

The Wind Obeys

Gabriela Banks
Adult Team Member

During our weeklong stay in King City, the weather often throws a wrench in our plans. The wind blows so hard from the north that all the trees in the park slant southward. We have to plan the adult afternoon craft very carefully to make sure the materials are heavy enough not to blow away. Being outside in such strong winds drains the energy we need to minister to our King City friends.

One year, dark clouds threatened to spoil our afternoon at the park. Just as the morning VBS was finishing up, someone asked me if we should move the picnic lunch indoors because it was already starting to sprinkle.

"No way," I said. "Let's just pray it away."

There have been times in my life when I just knew something

was or was not going to happen, and this was one of them. Since God had called us to minister to King City families at the park, I figured he would not sabotage his own plans. In that moment I was confident my thoughts were aligned with his and that all we needed to do was pray, and God would send the rain away. So we said a quick prayer, piled into cars, and drove to the park.

The student team members in my car were all talking about how it looked like it was going to rain and wondering what we would do if it did.

"It's not going to rain," I said firmly.

"Huh? How do you know?" asked the student who was riding shotgun.

"Because God called us to be here this week to serve the people of King City. We need to pray, and stand firm in the authority God gave us."

Again, I prayed in the name of Jesus Christ, commanding the rain clouds to leave, and asked God to bring us good weather that would not disrupt the plans he had for us that day. A few team members chuckled in agreement.

Thankfully, God used his power and authority over creation to move the rain clouds and we had a nice afternoon at the park. Weeks after that trip, the student who was in the front passenger seat of my minivan that afternoon mentioned the experience with the rain clouds at a small group meeting. I could tell it left an impression on him.

The following year on the first morning of the trip, the Saint John's VBS group and I gathered in a circle at Whisper Canyon to talk through the day and pray before heading into King City. Remembering how disruptive the wind usually is, I prayed for God to stop the wind so it wouldn't affect our afternoon. The group agreed with a raucous, "Amen!"

When we arrived at the park for lunch that day, I smiled because the wind wasn't blowing. There wasn't even a breeze. It seemed God had answered our prayer. I was sitting at a kids' craft table in the sun where student team members were helping kids braid lanyards and friendship bracelets. But the sun was so blazing hot I couldn't think clearly as I helped a six-year-old boy thread his lanyard. Adults walked around the kids' craft tables reminding everyone to drink lots of water so they wouldn't get dehydrated.

I kept thinking, *if only there was a slight breeze.* The little boy I was helping wandered off to play with a friend, so I took that as a cue to head for the shade. Then it dawned on me.

Oh, my goodness, we prayed the wrong prayer!

I quickly scanned the park for Steve, one of the adult team members from my morning huddle group. He was standing near the basketball court where he and a group of boys had just finished a game of hoops. I walked up to him and said, "Stevo, God answered our prayer for the wind to die down, but now it's too hot. I'm dying over there. We prayed the wrong prayer for such a hot day."

"Are you kidding? For once it was actually nice to play basketball because the wind wasn't tossing the ball all over the place during our game. It was really great!" He wiped the sweat off his face with his shirt sleeve. "But yeah, I hear you. It *is* pretty hot."

"There's no shade at any of the kids' craft tables. I was sitting over there practically melting. I mean, look at the trees. They're not even moving."

Steve laughed. "Yeah, I guess we prayed too hard this morning, huh? We should've prayed for a five-mile-an-hour breeze."

He was just joking, but I said, "Yes. That's a great idea. Let's do it!"

He struggled his shoulders. "Okay."

We closed our eyes, bowed our heads, and prayed. We

thanked God for hearing our prayer that morning and asked him to please bring a five-mile-an-hour breeze so that we could minister effectively to the kids.

I stood there in the shade talking to Steve about how well our new student team members were blending in. Two seniors who joined our outreach trip for the first time seemed to have no problem making connections with King City kids. All of a sudden, Steve looked behind him, extended his arms to the side, and then turned his head back around. “No way. Do you feel that?”

A gentle breeze had come up from behind him. I smiled as I felt the coolness on my forehead and neck, wet with sweat. I thought, *wow, that was quick!* But part of me also doubted the breeze would stay. I thought it was just a small gust that wouldn’t stick around. But as Steve and I stood there, the breeze remained consistent. I turned and looked over at the kids’ craft tables and could see a little girl’s long brown hair blowing ever so slightly in the breeze. Sure enough, a gentle breeze was making its way through the entire park. Steve’s eyes were so big and his mouth was wide open. “I can’t believe it. It’s about five miles per hour! That’s really cool.”

We both smiled ear to ear and praised God with high-fives. I walked back to the table to make more friendship bracelets and sat in the same spot where I was boiling before. Now I was perfectly comfortable. I sat there marveling at the wonder of the breeze and its cooling effects, and fully appreciating our gracious God.

The next day in our morning huddle at Whisper Canyon, I knew it was going to be another hot day so I made sure our huddle group prayed Steve’s way: for God to send a five mile an hour breeze.

After the morning VBS, our entire ministry team was sitting at the picnic tables in the park under the awnings. We were all enjoying our lunch break before setting up the afternoon activities.

Four high school boys who had been in my morning huddle group were looking at one of their cell phones and saying, "What? No way. Look at this!"

The student holding the phone called out to me. "Hey, Mrs. Banks! The weather app says the wind here in King City is 4.5 miles per hour!" He and all the guys around him laughed in amazement. "That's so cool!"

I smiled back at them, delighting at how playful God was being with all of us. I sat there in sheer amazement at how he heard each of our specific prayer requests. He didn't have to do that, but he answered us so clearly, so quickly, so tangibly, and he seemed to be having fun showing off his power.

I grinned and nodded my head as I felt God's immense love wrap around us with his gentle breeze. What a joy to see God making himself known to our students in this unique and tangible way.

I am the good shepherd...
My sheep hear my voice,
and I know them,
and they follow me. —John 10:14, 27

And Jesus came and said
to [the eleven disciples], "All authority in heaven
and on earth has been given to me.
Go therefore and make disciples of all nations,
baptizing them in the name of the Father
and of the Son and of the Holy Spirit,
teaching them to observe all that I have
commanded you." —Matthew 28:18-20

No longer do I call you servants,
for the servant does not know
what his master is doing;
but I have called you friends,
for all that I have heard from my Father
I have made known to you. —John 15:15

Chapter 15

One Small Step Leads to Deep Connections

Gail Nordby
Adult Team Member

It all started when I prayed, *Lord, use me today. Lead me to someone you want me to connect with, someone who needs to talk.* I'd been helping with the women's ministry for the week, but most of my time was spent explaining how to make the crafts. I longed for real connection with the women of King City.

That morning, as I was helping a woman named Doris understand how to do the craft, she received an important call from a hospital two-hours away from King City. Her 10-year-old daughter, Tracy, was suffering from unexplained seizures, and the hospital was calling to set up an appointment. I could see by her worried look that she was desperate to help her daughter.

As we talked, I learned that the family's house had burned to the ground a few months before Tracy got sick. Doris and her family were now living in temporary housing with another family. She had stopped working because Tracy was so sick, and the loss of her income was a strain on her family. My heart ached as I heard her story. I was overwhelmed by the depth of her suffering. I prayed, *God, how can I help this mom?*

I sensed him say, Listen, cry, and pray with her.

I was amazed at how God had placed me exactly where he wanted me, as my home was close to the Children's Hospital at Stanford where the appointment would be. I soon found out that Tracy just happened to be in the group of children my daughter, Sara, was ministering to. Sara was already building a relationship with Tracy and loved her. Sara's two friends, Cailley and Sarah, had also learned about Tracy's illness and had gotten to know her during VBS.

When Tracy's appointment finally came, doctors diagnosed Tracy with an aggressive form of cancer. The fight for Tracy's life started immediately with chemotherapy and radiation. We prayed constantly for her healing. Every Sunday afternoon during her treatment, our little group would visit Tracy and Doris, bringing them gifts and encouragement.

We felt God's presence many times while visiting them. One particular day, the girls brought Tracy a scrapbook they had made for her. It was filled with pictures of Tracy, her family, her friends, and Bible memory verses from the VBS camps we had attended together. Tracy and Doris were overwhelmed with joy to receive this gift because they had lost all their family pictures in the fire. With our girls surrounding her hospital bed, Tracy was determined to read each Bible verse and each word of encouragement by herself.

Tears streamed down our cheeks as we watched this determined, tired, little girl read the entire scrapbook page by page as if she couldn't get enough. That afternoon, God's words of hope spoke to all of us through a child's voice.

Months later, Tracy began responding to the treatment. In addition to physical healing in Tracy, we also noticed spiritual healing in the family. God was working mightily in Tracy and Doris's hearts and drawing their whole family closer to him. Doris started to read her Bible more often and talked to me about how she was seeking God and praying. He was hearing our prayers.

The relationships we built during this time were very dear. Tracy was able to go back home and continued to heal. That summer, the girls drove the two-hour journey to visit Tracy. She was doing much better and loved being home with her family. God's hand was on Tracy, Doris, and her family, and their faith continued to grow.

Four months later I received a phone call from Doris. Unbeknownst to us, Tracy's cancer returned in the fall and her health declined quickly. Doris was calling to tell us that Tracy had died at home surrounded by her family. Sara, Cailley, Sarah, and I were shocked and overcome with grief. The pain was so deep because we had all come to love Tracy and her family and had such hope for Tracy's healing. God had other plans for her. We felt privileged to attend Tracy's funeral, a celebration of her earthly life and her new life in God's presence. We were blessed to know that her family had the hope of Christ within them as well.

Looking back, I never could have imagined how God would answer my prayer that day or the journey he would take us on. God's plan began to unfold the minute I asked him to use me in King City. I then followed his lead step by step, not understanding the bigger picture of what would happen. All I was thinking about that day was making a connection with someone. My mind was so small compared to what he had in mind. I had no idea how deeply I would be touched by serving in King City or how God's hand would work through prayer. Although this experience was bittersweet, I praise God for how he blessed each of us through our relationships.

Each year when we go back to King City, we look forward to spending time with Doris and her family. The joy of seeing how God is working in their lives and healing them is so encouraging. Tears are still part of our conversations, but it's that tenderness that reminds us of Tracy and of the love we share.

The payment for sin is death, but
the gift that God freely gives is everlasting life
found in Christ Jesus our Lord. —Romans 6:23 GW

He will wipe away every tear from their eyes,
and death shall be no more,
neither shall there be mourning, nor crying,
nor pain anymore, for the former things
have passed away. —Revelation 21:4

We are more than conquerors through him
who loved us. For I am convinced that neither death
nor life, neither angels nor demons,
neither the present nor the future,
nor any powers, neither height nor depth,
nor anything else in all creation,
will be able to separate us from the love of God that is in
Christ Jesus our Lord. —Romans 8:37-39 NIV

To hear about a student's experience with this same King City family, be sure to read the next story by Sarah Lim entitled, "Little Things Make a Big Impact."

Chapter 16

Little Things Make a Big Impact

Sarah Lim
Student Team Member, 2013-2015
Student Team Leader, 2016

The first day I met Tracy[18] at VBS, she came up to me and started telling me story after story. Because of her illness, she couldn't be as active as the other children. So, while other campers ran around for hours, it was our mouths, rather than our legs, that moved nonstop.

Even though she was very sick, Tracy was overflowing with smiles and giggles and loved making duck faces. In spending a week with her, I discovered a ten-year-old girl who was just like me—she loved being around people, and people loved being around her.

Two weeks after returning from King City, I found out Tracy would be receiving treatments at the Children's Hospital at Stanford, which is near my home. I was excited by the opportunity to see her again. During her long hospital stay that summer, my friends and I visited her weekly and were able to build a relationship with her and her family. Our girl-talks and laughter over crazy selfies not only brightened Tracy's day but also illuminated mine.

Later that year during Christmas break, I received word of Tracy's passing. I was shocked because I had last heard that she was doing well. Despite the sadness I felt, I was also overcome with hope and an assurance that she was in heaven. Because of the confidence I have in the eternal life Jesus provides, I know death does not get the final word and I will see her again one day.

Through this experience, I got to see firsthand the impact little actions can have on others. My friends and I made a scrapbook for Tracy and gave it to her during her hospital stay. We did not think much of it, but now every time I talk to Tracy's mom, Doris, she brings out the scrapbook. She tells me how she shows it to everyone who comes and how much this book means to her. To us, the scrapbook was just a gesture of love and a gift to cheer Tracy up, but to Doris, it is so much more.

Getting to know Tracy fueled a desire in me to continue serving those who have less than I do by sharing the time and resources God has blessed me with. I still keep in touch with her family to this day. I love driving down to King City with friends during my college breaks. We spend the day with Tracy's siblings, cousins, and kids in the neighborhood, playing games at the park and ending the day eating pizza or tacos.

Through my friendship with Tracy, God tangibly showed me how he uses everything—even the seemingly worst moments in life—for his good. Before meeting Tracy, I knew this in my head but did not always take this message to heart in my day-to-day life. However, after getting to know Tracy, I now believe this without a doubt. Through her illness and death, I witnessed her family grow closer to each other and to God. Tracy truly showed me what it means to glorify God through even death—I've never met anyone as joyful as her despite the trials she faced daily. Tracy taught me the real-life impact love can have and I will always remember her.

And we know that for those who love God
all things work together for good,
for those who are called
according to his purpose. —Romans 8:28

He who raised the Lord Jesus
will raise us also with Jesus
and bring us with you
into his presence. —2 Corinthians 4:14

I've written this letter to you
who believe in the name of the Son of God
so that you will be assured and know
without a doubt that you have
eternal life. —1 John 5:13 TPT

Chapter 17

Wildfire at Whisper Canyon

Larry & Jennifer Lewis
Volunteer Caretakers of Whisper Canyon, 2010-2017

On the night of August 22, 2016, a California wildfire threatened to engulf Whisper Canyon Christian Camp in flames. Brush and trees in the area had been stressed by five years of drought, creating fuel for the fire.

The wildfire, named "Chimney Fire," started on August 13, six miles south of Whisper Canyon with Nacimiento Reservoir blocking its northward advance. A week later on Saturday, August 20, the fire was still on the south side of the Nacimiento Reservoir with winds blowing from the south. Even so, the Bryson Hesperia area, just west of Whisper Canyon, was under an evacuation order.

The next day, Sunday, August 21, we learned from Whisper Canyon neighbors, who stayed to defend their homes, that the flames were getting closer to camp and that one fire truck with four men began staging on-site at Whisper Canyon. We hoped the fire was veering to the northwest, but it appeared to be just one ridge away to the south.

That day, my wife, Jennifer, and I drove to Whisper Canyon to retrieve some items from the caretakers' house but couldn't get through. By that time Bryson Hesperia Road was closed and power in the surrounding had been turned off. When we got home that evening, I began asking for prayer that they would be successful in stopping the fire from reaching camp.

We needed a miracle.

Prayers began pouring in for God to spare our beloved campground. Members of our PBCC church body, staff at Mount Hermon Conference Center,[19] and Whisper Canyon neighbors prayed for our camp to be spared so it could continue to be used for God's kingdom purposes. We also prayed for God's presence to be at Whisper Canyon, for the Lord to blow the winds in miraculous ways to protect Whisper Canyon, and that God's mighty hand would rest on the ridge to prevent more flames from reaching the premises. We all prayed for a miracle to be seen by all and for God to receive glory and praise. That night the winds were calm and the humidity was high, but unfortunately, that did not stop the fire from progressing.

On Monday evening August 22, the fire crested the ridge to the south of the Whisper Canyon campground and was headed north toward our camp. It was also sweeping west, threatening Hearst Castle, then swerved back to the north and east. At about 10 p.m., the fire traversed up the south-facing slope of our campground and approached the camp's infrastructure. By that point, there were multiple fire engines stationed on the property. Their trucks covered our entire soccer field.

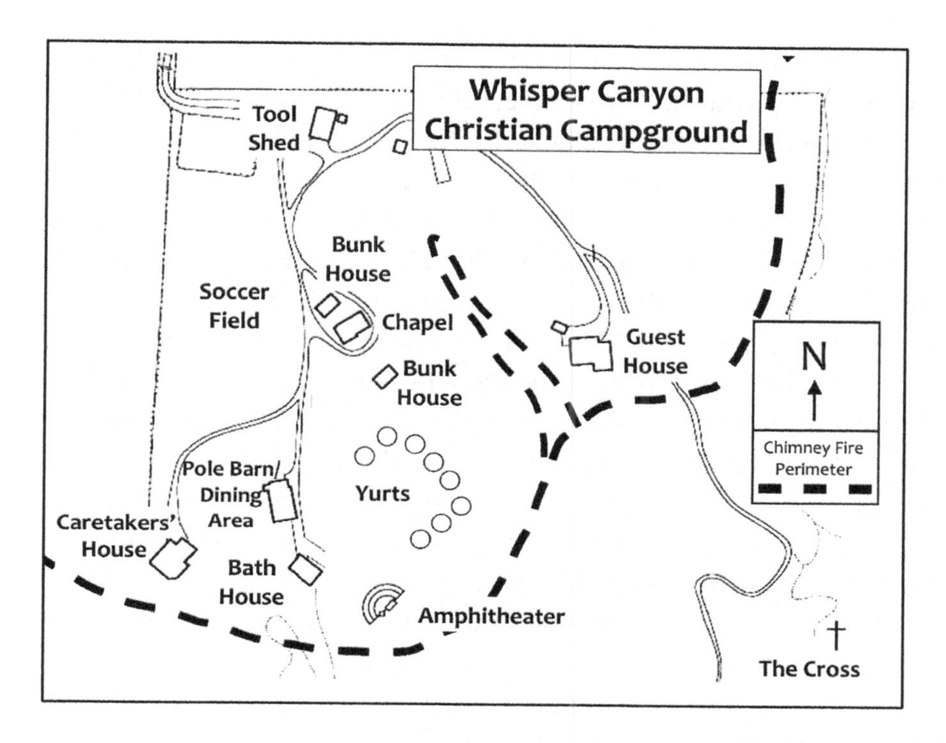

Firefighters applied Thermagel,[20] a fire retardant, to the back of the caretakers' unit to protect it from any flames that might touch the house. We found out later that they raided our tool shed and grabbed 18 shovels, a chainsaw, a sickle mower, and weed suppression equipment. With those tools, they cleared dry brush around the buildings and under the yurts,[21] ran the mower down the slope of the caretakers' house, and chopped down a dead oak tree before the fire charged up the slope. All their efforts made the camp defensible.

Fire crews also set a backfire[22] behind the caretakers' house, which reduced the flames to about 60 feet or so. Without that backfire, the flames would have been closer to 100 feet and the firefighters would have had to retreat. These backfires were set within minutes of the window of time to set them. That was miracle number one.

The fire then encircled two sides of the camp, sweeping north and east around the bathhouse, behind the yurts, and up behind the chapel. Firefighters backed a fire truck down the driveway of the caretakers' house and fought the 60-foot flames with their small tank of water using two fire hoses, one for each side of the house. All night long, fire crews held the flames at bay with only two fire hoses and that tank of water. Miracle number two.

At about 2 a.m. Tuesday morning, the fire progressed between the tool shed and the well, burning our neighbor's field but not damaging any of the structures. We lost some lumber but no equipment or buildings were damaged. Even the eight yurts, which have vinyl roofs and acrylic dome skylights, which could have blistered or melted from the fire's intense heat, were not harmed. Miracle number three.

The fire completely burned the hill with the white steel cross directly across from the camp's amphitheater. But both the cross itself and the wooden amphitheater were also completely unscathed. Miracles four and five.

The most significant miracle was the timing. If the fire had crested the ridge to the south in the morning, it would have raced up the slope to the camp in the heat of the day, overwhelming firefighters. The nighttime advance gave firefighters a better chance at containment. Our efforts at reducing the fuel load by trimming trees beforehand also helped. The hand crews borrowed shovels and rakes from the tool shed as well as the chainsaw. They used bulldozers to cut swaths back and forth, cutting through barbwire fences as needed. All this played a part but the real miracle was the timing.

The other factor that played a significant role was the soccer field. Without this level acre of clear space, the camp would have been indefensible. It gave the fire crews a safe place to park their vehicles off the roads while they fought the fire by hand without airplane support. Although they could have done so, fire crews did not sleep in the yurts but were on duty for 24-hour shifts.

In March of 2017, CalFire investigators concluded the Chimney Fire was caused by a vehicle that ignited dry grasses.[23] There were still spot fires for six weeks after the fire came through the camp. We could see spots glowing on the far hillside and could smell smoke well into September. But God was gracious in sparing our beloved campground, providing not just one miracle, but several. Clearly, he has further plans for this camp.

To God be the glory!

He who dwells in the shelter of the Most High
will abide in the shadow of the Almighty.
I will say to the LORD,
"My refuge and my fortress,
my God, in whom I trust."
For he will deliver you from the snare
of the fowler and from the deadly pestilence.
You will not fear the terror of the night,
nor the arrow that flies by day. —Psalm 91:1-3, 5

[Jesus said,] "If you abide in me, and if my words
abide in you, ask whatever you wish,
and it will be done for you." —John 15:7

Chapter 18

Renewed Energy

Melissa Brown
Student Team Member, 2015-2018

No matter how excited we are to play with and serve the kids of King City, my friends and I have always been exhausted after the third day of this trip. But this year God did something different.

On Tuesday after our long day in town, one of my friends who had collapsed on her bunk bed said to me, "I have no idea how I'm going to get through the rest of the week. I'm already so tired."

Five of us willingly start our days earlier than everyone else, putting in 17-hour days. We wake up at 5:30 a.m. to help make breakfast for the whole crew and get to bed at 10:30 p.m. During the hour-long drive from Whisper Canyon to King City, our carload of students is typically napping or chugging coffee to stay awake. This year in addition to exhaustion, most of the girls from my yurt were fighting severe congestion or coughing all week.

After the evening program each night, all the students meet in small groups around the campfire to talk and pray. That Tuesday night, we asked God to renew our strength so that we could serve the King City kids who never seem to run out of energy. The adults on the trip were also praying for us.

Wednesday is usually our hardest day. But not this year. At breakfast, nobody smiled brighter or cheered us on with more enthusiasm than my friend who didn't think she'd make it through the week. To my surprise, the people in my car were loudly singing Taylor Swift songs, telling funny stories from VBS the previous day, and even having deep conversations. The girls who were sick were the ones who played the hardest and were constantly surrounded by kids clamoring for their attention. They never ran out of energy.

I couldn't believe how God answered our prayers. My friends and I used Isaiah 40:30-31 all week, asking God for strength.

Even youths grow tired and weary,
and young men stumble and fall;
but those who hope in the LORD
will renew their strength.
They will soar on wings like eagles;
they will run and not grow weary,
they will walk
and not be faint. —Isaiah 40:30-31, NIV

I've never been on a King City trip where we weren't exhausted by Wednesday. Seeing my friends making it through the week with an amazing amount of energy on top of being sick was incredible. I found out later that Kyle, our youth pastor at the time, also experienced this renewed energy. He'd been staying up until 11:30 p.m. every night and waking up at 5:30 a.m. to make sure we were up to help cook breakfast, so by Tuesday he was exhausted. But when he woke up on Wednesday, he wasn't groggy; he felt joyful and excited, and even had enough energy to play sports in the late afternoon with the guys after a full day of VBS.

This experience reminds me that God loves it when we go out and help his people and that his is the higher power. It doesn't matter what Satan throws at us because God is constantly proving that nothing is impossible with him.

Fear not, I am the first and the last,
and the living one.
I died, and behold I am alive forevermore,
and I have the keys of Death
and Hades. —Revelation 1:17-18

Ah, Lord God!
It is you who have made the heavens
and the earth by your great power
and by your outstretched arm!
Nothing is too hard for you. —Jeremiah 32:17

I can do all things through him
who strengthens me. —Philippians 4:13

Chapter 19

The History of PBCC's King City Mission Trip

Ryan Hinn
Pastor, Peninsula Bible Church Cupertino

For nearly 30 years, the high school youth group of PBCC took its spring mission trip to Mexicali, Mexico. Heading into 2008, the plan remained the same. However, that spring was a little different.

Less than three weeks before we were supposed to leave for the trip, drug lords murdered someone near one of our ministry sites. A few days later, I and four other adult leaders met for lunch to discuss what we should do. As the new pastor on the staff, I had zero intention of pulling the plug on the trip. However, the other four leaders, veterans of the Mexicali outreach program, decided it was not wise to go to Mexico that year given that the cartel wars were intensifying. So we canceled the trip.[24]

We immediately began to brainstorm alternate options as we had essentially finished all the preparations for the trip, including having students clear their absences with their schools.

Jon Singley, one of the other adult leaders, and I began to connect with some people we knew at Mount Hermon Conference Center. Within 24 hours we secured a community to serve and a place to sleep. We would pitch our tents at Whisper Canyon Christian Camp, which was owned by Mount Hermon at the time, and we would present our VBS program to a church community in King City. Two days later, Jon, Ron Mills (another adult leader), and I took the two-hour drive to investigate the two sites.

Whisper Canyon, albeit a little overgrown with weeds, would be perfectly sufficient as a lodging spot. However, we needed to figure out how we would eat. Food for the Mexicali trip was always covered as a part of the program. But now that we were venturing out on our own, we had to find solutions for literally everything, including the food. Thankfully, we knew a married couple who had experience catering for large groups and who were willing to come along as our cooks. Chris and Cathy Gatley planned the menus, shopped for food, and cooked gourmet meals. Cathy continued to be our chef for the first ten years even though her youngest son had graduated nine years prior. She was a huge blessing to the trip.

As we drove into King City to scout out VBS options, the first point of contact was at Iglesia de Jesucristo. The pastor and his assistant were very welcoming and excited to have us bring our VBS to their church. Since we had three full teams of youth prepared for three separate VBS sites, we drove around town looking for other ministry opportunities. We dropped in at

Saint John the Baptist Catholic Church and were welcomed with open arms by the priest there. We continue to serve at this church where 200-300 elementary age kids join our VBS each year.

Over the decade, we have partnered with four different churches in King City: Iglesia de Jesucristo, Saint John's, First Baptist Church, and King City Bible Church. We have continued to build and maintain great relationships with the people and the leaders of these churches.

For the first several years, all of our teams would camp in tents. However, tent camping in that part of California in March and April is less than ideal—it rains. Sometimes it rains a lot. At the end of the trip a few years ago, after we'd had an abnormally wet week where several tents were sopping wet and surrounded by puddles of water, we spontaneously started a campaign to raise money for four yurts. That night, with cash and change from students, matching pledges from a number of adults, and a gift from King City Bible Church, we raised over $2,000.

What followed the next few months was even more incredible. It started with Mount Hermon agreeing to match up to $50,000 of donations to build four more yurts. Then, with a couple of people helping me spearhead a fundraising campaign, we raised $50,000 within three months. As promised, Mount Hermon matched that price, and someone from our church body "donated" money in the form of paying his construction crew to help build the foundations for the yurts. Over the course of the following 18 months, four yurts were built. Mount Hermon then paid for four more yurts. There are now eight yurts at Whisper Canyon Christian Camp,[25] providing comfortable (and dry) lodging for up to 80 people.

God has been very faithful to us. Not only did he bring the details of this first trip together in less than ten days, but he has also done so every year since 2008. Nearly every year, we have tweaked the schedule or added new ministry opportunities as needed—women's ministry, street cleaning, sports camp, a loaves and fishes food pantry program, and others. God miraculously created this trip and continues to bring life into it and out of it.

Countless lives have been touched by the gospel as a result of this trip. What you are reading in these pages gives testimony to just a small percentage of all the things God has done in the lives of countless students and adults over the first decade of the trip.

To God be the glory!

And he [Jesus] said to them,
"The harvest is plentiful, but the laborers are few.
Therefore, pray earnestly to the Lord of the harvest
to send out laborers into his harvest." —Luke 10:2

Faithful is He who calls you, and He also will
bring it to pass. —1 Thessalonians 5:24 NASB

Sing to the LORD, all the earth!
Tell of his salvation from day to day.
Declare his glory among the nations,
his marvelous works among all the peoples!
For great is the LORD,
and greatly to be praised, and he is to be feared
above all gods. —1 Chronicles 16:23-25

Chapter 20

Overcoming Fear to Pray for Healing

Gabriela Banks
Adult Team Member

On the last day at camp, I kept pleading silently to God. *If I step out in faith and pray with Esperanza, will you heal her?*

I met Esperanza and her husband while serving with the women's crafts on my first trip to King City in 2016. I felt a bond with them immediately—their warm greetings, genuine hospitality, and gentle smiles reminded me of my aunts and uncles in Mexico, who I adore.

A few years later, Esperanza came to women's crafts cradling her injured elbow, which she'd broken two months earlier. The craft that morning involved cutting out magazine pictures and gluing them to the cover of a blank journal. With her left arm tucked into her side, she struggled to cut out the pictures one-handed. Moving her arm was extremely painful.

Seeing my friend this way made my heart heavy, so I immediately sat next to her to help her cut and glue as we caught up on life. She said surgeons tried repairing the break by putting a metal plate in her arm but left her arm immobilized and in so much pain that she had to leave her job. She stopped going to physical therapy because when therapists moved her arm, it caused excruciating pain. Cooking and doing household chores were now a huge challenge. I grieved for her as I pictured her trying to cook over a hot stove with one hand while holding her other arm against her body to avoid pain.

As I sat with her, I prayed silently. *Lord, if I pray with her, will you heal her arm?*

I've been involved in healing prayer for several years and have seen injuries healed; some spontaneously, and some gradually over time. But I don't always know *for sure* if God will actually heal someone before I pray for them. I desperately wanted to pray with Esperanza for healing, but I hesitated because I didn't want to give her false hope. *What if she doesn't experience any improvement? Will she be disappointed?*

So I kept pleading with God. *Lord, she needs to work to help support her family. Will you please heal her if I offer to pray with her?*

I paused and waited for a reply, even a hint. But his silence persisted. And so did my inner turmoil. Having grown up in a low-income family, I remember how much stress my parents endured as they worried how they were going to pay the bills, especially when one of them was out of work due to an illness or hospitalization. My heart went out to Esperanza and her husband as I imagined what they might be facing in a similar situation.

Later that afternoon, I saw her again at the park. She and her family smiled and waved as they walked toward the craft table. Once again, my strong desire to pray for her surged inside me. *This is our last day in King City. If I don't pray for her now, I'll miss the opportunity to see if God will heal her. But if I pray and he doesn't heal her, well then, I can have peace knowing I tried. I can at least show her the love and compassion I'd want someone to show me if I were in her shoes.*

I invited my friend Eli, who also has experience with healing prayer, to join me. His "yes" gave me the boldness to approach Esperanza. I told her, "I've seen people healed of pain and injuries, but we never know what God will do or what his timing is for healing." She agreed wholeheartedly, saying, *"Dios es soberano y su tiempo es perfecto."* (God is sovereign and his timing is perfect.) Her response put my heart at ease.

We sat next to her at the craft table with her husband on the other side and began to pray. We prayed and spoke softly to Esperanza so as not to draw extra attention to ourselves. Her pain was a five on a scale from zero to ten while her arm was perfectly still. We prayed in the name of Jesus several times for the pain and trauma to leave and we anointed her with oil.

My worst fears of her not being healed were coming true. But we weren't done, and neither was God.

After about twenty minutes with no improvement whatsoever, Eli and I asked God, "What's standing in the way of her healing?" As we listened, God highlighted to both Eli and me individually that we were both distracted by a spirit of fear because we were praying in a public place. Very true. Even though everyone else around us was busy making the necklace craft and not paying attention to us, we felt vulnerable to criticism praying in this setting.

We then prayed against the spirit of fear and sensed peace. We prayed for Esperanza again, and her pain level went down from a five to a three. We praised God and were surprised by what happened next.

When I laid hands on Esperanza (with her permission), I felt heat on her elbow. We all took turns feeling it and we knew it was a sign that God was at work because her elbow wasn't just warm like when inflammation is present. It was hot. And the heat was only at the site of the main injury on her elbow. We all rejoiced, thanking God for loving her in this way.

But progress on reducing her symptoms stalled. She still could not lift her arm without pain. About forty-five minutes into this prayer, Eli felt we were supposed to continue contending for her. Esperanza appreciated our efforts, so we asked God how to proceed. After a few minutes of listening prayer, I sensed Esperanza might need to forgive the doctors for the botched surgery and the physical therapists for hurting her. She agreed and did so willingly.

When we prayed again, she started to feel the pain lessen. I thanked God and encouraged her to try lifting her arm. I asked God to release any tension in her shoulder and slowly but surely, she began raising her arm above her head with little pain. She still had a slight bend in her elbow because the metal plate was restricting her movement. But as we pressed in for her healing, her pain continued to decrease until it was 100 percent gone.

We were all overcome by God's love for her and celebrated with high fives, hugs, and tears. I snapped a picture of Esperanza smiling and holding the long necklace string with her arms wide open. She was able to string the beads with no assistance.

Five months later when I visited Esperanza and her husband in King City, I was pleased to hear her healing had continued. The only time she had pain in her elbow was when lifting something heavy or when it's cold outside. She regained her mobility, had not returned to the physical therapist, and was still free of pain for daily activities.

She also told me that after the accident, she'd been afraid of falling again and re-injuring herself. After we prayed for her, her fear of falling disappeared along with the pain. Hearing this news brought me such joy. We rejoiced together and praised God for his overwhelming love for Esperanza and how he had made his tangible presence known to her.

Looking back at this experience, I'm struck by my perception of God's "silence." Maybe God wasn't silent at all but was "speaking" to me through my heart of compassion for my friend. As I practice hearing God more clearly, I'm reminding myself that he can speak through all of our senses, and even through those compassionate tugs on our hearts. I'm also struck by how God kept answering us as we pressed into him and asked more questions. This reminds me not to give up so quickly when I pray for myself or others, but to keep engaging God with conversational, listening prayer, and to practice listening for his voice.

It is the glory of God to conceal things,
but the glory of kings
to search things out. —Proverbs 25:2

Surely he has borne our griefs
and carried our sorrows;
yet we esteemed him stricken,
smitten by God, and afflicted.
But he was pierced for our transgressions;
he was crushed for our iniquities;
upon him was the chastisement
that brought us peace, and with his wounds
we are healed. —Isaiah 53:4-5

After this the Lord appointed seventy-two others
and sent them on ahead of him,
two by two... And he said to them,...
"Heal the sick and say to them,
'The kingdom of God has
come near to you.'" —Luke 10:1, 2, 9

Chapter 21

Transforming Lives through Baseball & Teamwork

George Stoyko
Adult Team Leader since 2000

In the 20 years I've been going on the PBCC outreach trip, first to Mexicali and then to King City, I've seen God transform the lives of those we serve, PBCC and WGBC teens and adults, and my own children.

I've been leading the baseball ministry since 2003. Our goal with baseball is to minister to the whole person by addressing their spiritual, physical, intellectual, and emotional well-being. Each afternoon, after playing baseball for forty-five minutes, we take a snack break and use that time to engage the kids in a relaxed conversation about Bible lessons from the morning VBS program. We ask questions in small groups to learn about their family life, their understanding of spiritual things, and their hopes for the future. The casual atmosphere helps kids feel comfortable and gives them the confidence to express their spiritual concerns and search for answers. We pray for their individual needs before heading back out to the field for more baseball fun.

I enjoy seeing kids who will probably never play organized baseball learn to throw, catch, and hit a baseball. One year, a boy whose left arm was malformed from a birth defect joined us. At first, his mom pulled him out of the group because she was afraid he'd fail and be disheartened. But after I talked with her through an interpreter, she allowed him to join us and he played with the biggest smile, especially when getting a hit. Nothing is better than seeing the joy on the boys' and girls' faces when they get a hit or catch a fly ball! Praising every good effort builds self-esteem and emotional confidence that extends beyond the baseball field.

Over the years, I've noticed some of these positive effects on the kids who participate. Both King City kids and PBCC/WGBC students need space to relax, enjoy the company of others, and feel that they are making a contribution to a team's success or an individual player's growth and improvement. King City kids love the attention of our teens, and our teens love the affection they receive in return. With busy older siblings and parents sometimes working long hours, parenting can be challenging because of the pressure their children face to join a gang, which can portray a false sense of belonging. But having King City kids interact with our teens who are growing spiritually shows them the possibility of belonging to God's family, giving them a redemptive alternative to joining a gang.

Some of the King City teens who once played baseball with us but are too old for the VBS program still spend time with us in the park or stop by to talk with me. I've had the opportunity to reconnect with several of them who are now attending or have graduated from high school. We talk about real issues they face, such as struggling in school, having a parent whose cancer has returned, being followed by gang members when leaving work at night, or recognizing their own rebellion and its effect on their relationship with their parents. Getting to listen to and pray with them is a privilege that comes from having served them and gaining their trust.

As an adult team member, I have observed our PBCC/WGBC teens come in as freshmen a little reserved. As they progress through their high school years, many of them change and grow deeper in their relationship with God, gaining confidence as they grow. When sharing their stories, they talk about their journaling, the hard year they had, and how God brought them through it. As with the King City kids, it's been a privilege for me to pray with some of them and encourage them in their walk with Christ.

I believe their growth is enhanced by their involvement in this team ministry, with older students leading younger ones in being vulnerable and with adult leaders modeling vulnerability and supporting them. These mission trips have shown me how God uses all parts of the body of Jesus to display his character and to draw others to himself. God blesses team ministries in unique ways, and that blessing is both for us and for others. Some people are better at ministering to the teens, and I learn a lot by observing them. Others are better at guiding us as a spiritual community. All of us have different gifts, and God intended it that way so that no one of us can be everything to everybody. We all need each other and we need all the gifts.

The overall impact I have seen with this outreach trip is what Jesus spoke of when he said, “By this all people will know that you are my disciples, if you have love for one another” (John 13:34-35). Having a safe and trustworthy church community allows us to be vulnerable with each other. This ability to share deep and personal struggles leads us to have compassion and understanding for one another, which tightens the bonds in our community. Seeing this love at work in and through our teens and adults naturally draws King City kids to us and to Jesus.

Year after year, the trip shows me how God is still at work in the lives of teens and reminds me to be faithful in praying for them. It also makes me want to continue to be a part of the transforming work God is doing through the King City ministry—he is faithful in moving us to be more like Jesus. And in that movement, he is calling others to follow Jesus with us.

A new command I give you:
Love one another. As I have loved you,
so you must love one another.
By this everyone will know that you are
my disciples, if you love
one another. —John 13:34-35 NIV

There are different kinds of gifts,
but the same Spirit distributes them....
Now to each one the manifestation of the Spirit
is given for the common good....
Just as a body, though one,
has many parts, but all its many parts
form one body, so it is
with Christ. —1 Corinthians 12:4, 7, 12 NIV

Chapter 22

Receiving More Than I Give

Sofia Rebsamen
Adult Team Member

I volunteered to help with women's crafts in King City even though I'm terrible at them. I figured I could be useful because I was born and raised in Mexico City, my first language is Spanish, and I share a common culture with the people there. I wanted to serve others by giving them my time and attention. Because I have a comfortable life in Silicon Valley, I assumed I would have much to offer someone who works in the fields harvesting produce. But I was so wrong. Through the people of King City, God showed me what it really means to give.

I've gone on this trip twice. And even though I only stayed for two days on my first trip and one day on my second trip, I have come to love the people of King City. The first year I was there, a King City mom confided in me and shared personal stories about her family's struggles. A friend joined me to talk and pray with her. And I thought, who am I to deserve to hear such a personal story? Without really knowing me, she trusted me enough to tell me her story and invite me into her life. In doing so, she taught me a lesson of love with her example—that she trusts me, a stranger but fellow believer, simply because we are sisters in Christ.

When we go to King City, families take the time to cook for us. Once they brought us homemade *tamales*, and another time, homemade *buñuelos*, both of which take a lot of time and effort to cook. They often choose one day to serve a homemade lunch to our entire team of 70 or so people. They are always happy to see us and they make us feel so at home.

I went there to make them feel loved and close to God, but they are the ones, with their genuine hearts, laughter, and gifts of food, who serve me. I might bring them a slice of cake as a gift, but they bring us an entire pan of flan. They are so willing to share what they have with me, and they love me because of who they are, not because of who I am. They give out of sincere love, and no money can repay what they offer.

When I first volunteered to go on this trip, I was willing to give up two days of my time and drive two hours away to invest in their lives. To me, that was a sacrifice, and I was eager to participate. But then I learned that my new King City friends would miss work just to talk with me because I was only there for two days. I realized if they don't go to work, they don't get paid. And yet, they would rather sit and talk with me because I'm a visitor from out of town.

In our fast-paced, work-comes-first, Silicon Valley culture, we don't think of taking a day off to come to an event like this because we could earn a day's wages instead. Pressures at work and our individualistic culture makes it difficult for us to go out of our way to make room in our schedule for people. But King

City families are so ready to do it. It's very powerful how they love.

Through my King City friends, God is teaching me a lesson by telling me, "See, this is what I mean when I say we are family. We are vulnerable with one another, we trust one another, we confide in one another, and we sacrifice real time for one another." These loving people are showing me what Jesus would do. They are teaching me what it means to love, what it means to serve, and what it means to have fellowship and grace because they are gracious enough to trust in me. But who am I to deserve it? I'm no one. Yet they say I am. And that's how God works. It's not us or them but God himself giving us grateful hearts for one another's lives.

In the end, God turned my perspective upside down. My King City friends ended up being my example. I thought I was going to serve them, but I'm the one who's on the receiving end. I thought I would bless them, but they have blessed me much more and I'm receiving way more than I give. I thought I was supposed to teach, but I'm the one getting the lesson on how to love.

And it turns out that being bilingual was not important. It wasn't my skills that God wanted to use, but my whole self and what I have to offer just by being there with them. In the kingdom of God, what's needed are people with willing hearts to love.

If I speak in the tongues of men or of angels,
but do not have love,
I am only a resounding gong
or a clanging cymbal.
Follow the way
of love. —1 Corinthians 13:1; 14:1 NIV

Whoever brings blessing will be enriched,
and one who waters will himself
be watered. —Proverbs 11:25

But we have this treasure in jars of clay
to show that this all-surpassing power
is from God and not
from us. —2 Corinthians 4:7 NIV

Chapter 23

Uninhibited Praise & Worship

Gabriela Banks
Adult Team Member

It was the final day of the 2018 King City trip. The entire ministry team sat under the morning sun on the wooden benches of Whisper Canyon's amphitheater listening to testimonies of how the Lord made his tangible love known to us all week.

Shea described how God used hip-hop dance to help him overcome anxiety. Melissa marveled at how he miraculously restored team members from exhaustion. Brian choked back tears as he recounted how God answered the team's prayers for his wife and unborn baby so he could return to minister. We listened to story after story while gazing across the canyon at the white cross and rows of mountains in the distance. After each testimony of God's personal love, everyone applauded and cheered, filling the air with a sweet fragrance of joy and gratitude.

Later that evening, most of the ministry team returned to this spot for an optional last night of student-led worship by the campfire. Daphne and Bella were standing next to each other in the front row of the amphitheater smiling, singing, and dancing to the music. No one could tell by looking at these graduating seniors how much strife they'd overcome in their relationship.

During their early years in high school, a weighty conflict had driven a wedge between them. I'd heard hints about their disagreement, how they'd been close friends since grade school, but how they were no longer speaking to each other. Several of us had been praying for God to restore their friendship.

The week before this trip, when Bella finished sharing her testimony with our team, Cindi, the small group leader, looked around the circle of 30 or so students and asked, "Who'd like to pray for her?" Daphne raised her hand, got up, and stood behind Bella. Placing her hands on Bella's shoulders, Daphne bowed her head, thanking God for Bella, how he had worked so powerfully in her life and asked him to continue watching over her. After the prayer, Bella stood up and turned around. These two girls embraced each other in a long, tight hug as tears flowed down their cheeks. I wiped my eyes, utterly amazed at how God had fully reconciled this friendship.

Now here they were standing shoulder to shoulder in front of the campfire with the rest of us, praising God together. My son Lucas, now a senior, was leading the worship team. As I looked around and locked my eyes on individual faces glowing in the firelight, memories flooded my mind of Lucas and his classmates as chubby-cheeked toddlers learning "Jesus Loves Me" for the first time in Sunday school. They then became rambunctious middle-schoolers who couldn't stay quiet or still in small group. Here they all were, singing praise songs by the campfire, many of them graduating seniors about to head off to college. The energy and excitement in the air was palpable. We stood on the amphitheater benches rather than sitting, basking in the sheer delight of all God had done throughout the week.

I smiled, marveling at how much they had matured and grown in the Lord and how much freedom several of these students had recently experienced. Daphne and Bella's story, along with thirty other testimonies shared earlier that day, were great reasons to celebrate.

Lucas and the band asked everyone to call out songs for them to play. Students started off the night requesting children's songs they'd sung at VBS such as, "The Lord's Army,"[26] "O Happy Day,"[27] and "Big House."[28] They all laughed together as they sang and did the hand motions. They also requested more contemplative praise songs like "Called Me Higher,"[29] "King of My Heart,"[30] and "Here As in Heaven."[31]

We sang along loudly as if we were at a rock concert, some of us with arms raised. The crowd expressed so much love and joy that night along with deep appreciation for the powerful God we serve.

At one point, a few of us requested "Reckless Love,"[32] a song about the immense love of God and how he leaves 99 others to fiercely fight just for us. During that song, Daphne, Bella, and other girls in the front row spontaneously created hand motions for the bridge. They threw their legs up in karate kicks and punched the air with their fists to emphasize how God relentlessly lights up shadows, scales mountains, and knocks down walls that try to separate us from him. I'll never forget the grit on these girls' faces as they praised God.

Although there were a few people in the crowd who worshipped more inwardly than the rest of us, the overall mood that evening was exuberance mixed with moments of heartfelt worship. Inspired by our high-spirited praise, I got the idea to teach students how to wave worship flags, colorful pieces of fabric used to express appreciation or joy to the Lord during worship. I used to despise worship flags until God taught me about uninhibited praise[33] by reminding me how King David danced with all his might in the streets of Jerusalem (2 Samuel 6:5, 14). Introducing the flags was a natural extension to the worship we were already exhibiting. So as the music continued, I stepped down next to the band, demonstrated how to wave a flag, and invited a few students to try it.

At first, most of them shook their heads, not interested, possibly because it was a foreign concept to them. But the awkwardness soon left as I brought out a second flag and encouraged pairs of students to wave them side by side. Members of the band and a few people in the stands shouted out for us to move back behind the fire pit so they could see us in the light of the campfire. Pairs of students took turns dancing with the flags and then handed them to other students at the end of each song.

I noticed that students waved the flags in ways that reflected their unique personalities. Bella spun around with elegant dance moves, while Daphne used her athletic skills to twirl the flag left and right. Shea, the hip-hop dancer, asked to use both flags at the same time, spinning them both above his head with quick and rhythmic moves as if he'd done so for years. We all erupted in shouts of amazement at his skill. He told me afterward that his experience with martial art sticks made waving the flags easy. When a pair of boys flung the flags like swords in swift and sharp cutting moves, everyone laughed and cheered them on.

As I watched student after student waving the flags in the light of the campfire, I was struck by the incredible amount of freedom they displayed. They praised God with uninhibited joy, laughter, and exuberance. Our celebration felt so genuine. We were having a party *with* Jesus and *for* Jesus. What a privilege to witness this freedom unfold and to celebrate together as the family of God!

At the end of the worship session when all the VBS children's songs had been sung, and the flags became normalized, the focus shifted back to the cross. The very last song these students requested to sing was "No Longer Slaves."[34] The song points to the truth that because Jesus conquered death, we are no longer slaves to sin, but are the chosen children of the Most High God.

The mood shifted naturally from crazy laughter and loud shouts to heartfelt thanks to God for his work in us. The two students holding the flags waved them slowly to the beat, getting lost in the lyrics while staring at the flames. As we sang "No Longer Slaves" together, we proclaimed our true identity as Father God's rescued sons and daughters, no longer in bondage to fear. I looked over at Bella and Daphne who were swaying back and forth in the firelight. What a joy to see them worshiping God in their newfound freedom.

My heart overflowed with appreciation and gratitude for how God was tenderly wooing these kids to himself and making his love so tangible and accessible to them. I myself didn't understand the full meaning of the cross until my late 30's. Imagine how much farther these kids will grow in their faith because they're experiencing Jesus' resurrection power at such a young age. Thinking about this and watching them openly profess their love and appreciation for Jesus' work on the cross moved me to tears.

Like the finale of a fireworks show, singing "No Longer Slaves" fired a row of exclamation points at the end of our trip. It was powerful and fitting to end with this song after all the freedom our ministry team had collectively tasted and seen. How beautiful to behold new levels of freedom in praise and worship in these teenagers, and what a privilege to worship alongside them and to celebrate the Lord's work as a church family.

Generation after generation will declare
more of your greatness
and declare more of your glory.

Your magnificent splendor
and the miracles of your majesty
are my constant meditation.

Your awe-inspiring acts of power
have everyone talking!
I'm telling people everywhere
about your excellent greatness!

You're kind and tenderhearted to
those who don't deserve it
and very patient with people who fail you.
Your love is like a flooding river
overflowing its banks
with kindness. —Psalm 145:4-6, 8 TPT

III. GRAFTED INTO THE KINGDOM

Oh, taste and see
that the LORD is good!
Blessed are those
who take refuge in him!
—Psalm 34:8

By this my Father is glorified,
that you bear much fruit and so prove
to be my disciples.
—John 15:8

Chapter 24

Preparing for Re-entry: Simple Strategies That Work

After living in an environment for a week where God's love is so tangible, it's easy for team members to experience an "after-camp crash" when they return to their busy routines at home. So on the last night of one of the King City trips, David Misson, a youth pastor at Willow Glen Bible Church, made a point to help students transition from the "camp high" to normal life.

Ask Strategic Questions

As we were all sitting in the amphitheater overlooking the campfire, David asked strategic questions to help them think about what they could do to avoid the after-camp crash. His first question was, "Why is it easier for you to experience God on the

King City mission trip than it is at home?" After a few minutes of silence, they responded,

- It's hard to see God in everyday rituals of school. I'm ready to see God here in King City and Whisper Canyon, but I'm not expecting to see him at home.
- We have time to pause and reflect here on the trip, but there's no time to do that at home.
- It's hard to notice God in the public school setting.
- We're intentional about telling our King City friends about God, but not so at home.
- The body of Christ comes together here.
- I don't think of how God is working at home, so I don't share it.
- At camp, God is the focus, but at home, homework is the focus.
- Here, there's a willingness to be friendly because we're serving and that's the mindset. But at home, I'm not in that mindset.

David then asked, "What are the elements here that could be part of your life at home? In other words, what do you do here that you could do at home?" Students replied,

- Join a small group and attend it regularly.
- Be open and vulnerable with each other like we are here.
- Do a better job of affirming each other more often like we do in the affirmation circle on the last day at Whisper Canyon.
- Keep hugging people at home, loving each other and loving God, and the rest will fall into place.

- Take time to reflect on what God did here in King City so we can remember how God is faithful.
- Share our testimonies with people.
- Encourage one another to read the Bible and stay connected to community, especially the one we've built here.
- Challenge ourselves to see God and ask each other, "How did you see God in your life today?"
- Expect God to show up in our lives at home.

One of the adult volunteers raised her hand. "You guys are always on your smartphones. You could actually use SnapChat to ask each other how you saw God in your day." Everyone laughed out loud. One student said, "True!"

Empower Teens to Take the Lead

"These are all great ideas," David said. "You all need each other once you get back home. It will take more effort to do these things once you get back into your routine, so walk out of here with a plan. Be proactive about putting some of these things into place. Some of you need to step up and do something about it." David encouraged them to learn how to make God a priority in their lives at home because many things compete for their time and attention.

When David dismissed the group, a few students stayed by the campfire to chat about what he had said. A few months after they returned from that trip, groups of students actually took the re-entry advice to heart.

Student-led Re-entry Activities

"The God Squad." Eight students from Monta Vista High School started thinking about how to connect with God at school and support each other in their faith. Allen Iwamoto, a junior at the time, suggested they meet every Tuesday and Thursday during brunch to talk about how they notice God working in their lives and to share prayer requests.

"The God Squad," the name they gave themselves, gathered on bleachers next to the swimming pool to eat, catch up with each other, and read the Bible verse of the day. They ended their time together in huddle formation for a quick prayer before heading back to class. When interviewed about the God Squad in a short video documentary, Maddi Marten, a senior that year, said, "I feel closer to God when I'm with other people who are encouraging me to grow in my faith."

SnapChat Fellowship. Another group of students began using SnapChat to keep in touch the rest of that school year and during the summer before the seniors left for college. "We realized we didn't have to *only* talk about God at church and on mission trips," said Allison Lee. "We could do it in SnapChat, in a text, or over boba." Students would start their SnapChat messages to each other with the acronym, "HDYSGWIYLT," which referred to the question, "How did you see God work in your life today?"

Looking back on the SnapChat group, Allison said, "I was blessed by those conversations because we shared how God moved in hard things and some fun things, too. Instead of just asking, 'How are you today?' the acronym reminded us to be thankful and reflective. And even though we all go to different colleges, we still meet up and pick up where we left off. We're more than just friends because of our tight fellowship."

Staying Connected to God and One Another

Thanks to the action items generated by David's re-entry exercise, these students left Whisper Canyon equipped and inspired to stay connected to God and to each other. In fact, all of the students who were in the God Squad and SnapChat groups got plugged into a Christian group on campus their freshman year in college and are still involved in a Christian community.

Although these positive results may not necessarily happen with every group of students, our youth group experienced positive outcomes with this intentional approach. Of course, this re-entry strategy isn't the only way to encourage students in their faith. As you read in Chapter 2, the design of this outreach program helps foster long-term faith.

Regardless of *why* students are staying connected to Christian communities, the fact that they're plugged into college fellowship groups is significant in this day and age given that 64% of young people disconnect from their Christian communities between the ages of 18 and 30.[35] Students who participate in King City mission trips and who are encouraged to be intentional about seeking God and supporting one another's spiritual journeys, are well-placed to continue pursuing their faith in college and beyond.

Chapter 25

Changing the Spiritual Atmosphere

Letters from King City Community Leaders

Every year when we go to King City, we interact with local pastors and community leaders. Listen to what these community leaders say about how Jesus is using our VBS program to change the spiritual atmosphere and transform hearts.

— • —

Dear PBCC,

Spring break of 2019 marked the eleventh year our church and community received the blessings of your ministry. While I have only been the pastor of the First Baptist Church for the last six years, I can assure you that we are very grateful for the work and sacrifice of your students.

Our church community has directly benefitted each year from the work you do at the various sites in King City, including the sports camp and clothing distribution. Our children have been blessed by the teaching and activities and by relationships that have developed with your students. Most of the children who participate in your sports camp acquire skills and have a lot of fun they would not otherwise have an opportunity to receive. Your example has also inspired some in our church to organize a summertime VBS for the last two years.

Your presence in King City brings a sense of affirmation to our small community. It is easy to feel overlooked and neglected in South Monterey County as the ebb and flow of services comes into our area only to be withdrawn during times of economic decline. But you have been consistent and faithful to this ministry despite the roller coaster of state financial movement. Your efforts to come and minister year after year affirms the worth and value of our small church and King City's impoverished community.

It is my belief that there will be many in heaven as a result of this PBCC student ministry. It is my prayer that the time spent in your student outreach program will develop a new generation of ministers, mission-minded laypersons, and missionaries. May God continue to bless your church family and the ministry to youth and college-age students according to his riches in glory.

Sincerely,

Pastor Ken Reese
First Baptist Church
King City, CA

~ ~ ~

Dear Peninsula Bible Church Cupertino,

I want to share my perspective on the positive impacts I have seen from your church's yearly trips to King City.

As a former city councilwoman and 40-year resident of King City, I have long believed in the power of people of faith to bring good things to a community, but it wasn't until I saw for myself the joyful noises of school children playing with your teens that I realized something special was going on here.

Spring break is a time when parents need activities for their children so your program comes at a perfect time. In our agricultural community, many of the parents in our town have two income-earners who work in order to make ends meet, so finding positive opportunities for their children while they are working is important to them.

I am impressed with the way your program unites the denominations in our town–hosting events at a Catholic and Baptist church, inviting members from the Spanish-language church Iglesia De Jesucristo, welcoming those without a church affiliation and those of other denominations to participate.

The laughter of children playing games, the sounds of joyful music and Bible story skits, the craft activities for mothers, and the afternoon sports program that utilizes our local San Antonio Park all bring about a sense of excitement and enjoyment for the students who attend and for those in town who witness the event. It helps teach that the body of Christ extends beyond the borders of where we live, and the atmosphere that week promotes the idea that the Christian life can and should be one of joy and friendship.

I have also witnessed service projects by your teens over the years as they pulled weeds from our main street, removed litter and debris from our San Lorenzo Creek basin, cleaned up a school garden, and distributed clothing donated by your PBCC members. All these things are examples of Christians showing love for strangers. The world needs more of this. Thank you PBCC for your incredible gift to King City.

Karen Jernigan
King City, CA

~ ~ ~

Dear PBCC,

When members of your church first arrived in King City in 2008 with Bible stories and sports games for our youth and children, and creative art projects for our mothers and teens, members of our community wanted to know who had come and why. They were happy to hear that young people and adults came to share the love of Jesus with us and they asked when you would be back. They became very excited to hear you would be returning the following year.

Our community has come to know that each year the *güeros* (young American boys and girls full of joy and enthusiasm eager to serve) will be coming each year to present fun activities. As the years have passed, we have noticed and appreciated your consistency in coming to love our community.

The children tell us they've made new friends with your youth and they want you to come back soon. Parents who continually ask me who the *güeros* are and why they come tell me they feel safe having their children play with the trustworthy PBCC youth.

The hearts of our young people who witness your loving acts of service have been deeply touched—we have noticed positive changes in their behavior toward their parents and the community. Other parents tell me their kids want to go to church here in King City. These parents and young people in our church and in the larger King City community also ask me to thank you for what you do.

We have been so impressed to see the talents and willingness of each person who carries out these events, especially the youth who sacrifice their time to serve. Your young people have been an inspiration for us to serve as well.

We want you to know how important your spiritual influence is in bringing the blessings of God to our community. At different times, God lifts up a body of people who can help in different areas. We appreciate you and especially the fact that you have been coming to our city every year since 2008. Your consistency is because God's hand is on you. Otherwise, if it were not of God, you would have stopped coming here.

We also want you to know that we are praying for you—for God to give you grace in what you say and in what you do and that he will protect you.

May God greatly bless each of you at PBCC who make the events possible.

Sincerely yours,

Pastor Arturo Ríos
Iglesia de Jesucristo
King City, CA

IV. NEW WINE

No one puts new wine into old wineskins.
If he does, the wine will burst the skins—
and the wine is destroyed,
and so are the skins.
But new wine is for fresh wineskins.
—Mark 2:22

New growth is fragile;
nurture it gently,
cultivate it purposefully.
Every testimony a precious gift
from our Heavenly Father,
for us to taste and see
his extravagant love.
Every story a window
into the Father's heart for us,
his beloved children.
Every divine encounter
a glimpse of heaven on earth.
Nurture new growth gently.
Treasure it deeply.
Cultivate it purposefully.
Prayerfully.

Chapter 26

Nurturing New Spiritual Growth

This whole thing was and is God's idea. He intentionally chose King City, purposefully moving our mission trip from Mexicali to this hard-working agricultural community. He heard the cries of his people and he is sending teens and adults from Peninsula Bible Church Cupertino and Willow Glen Bible Church to love them and bring them the good news of the gospel of Jesus Christ.

The cool thing is, those of us who volunteer on these outreach trips are being transformed as we serve. Students and adults alike are growing in their faith and learning to notice God in their everyday lives, causing these weeklong trips to have more than a one-week impact. And one thing is clear—Jesus is here!

The Messiah has landed. He is the same yesterday, today, and forever. We've experienced his presence. Jesus is the power source in each of these stories. We can't untaste or unsee all he has done and is doing.

We have witnessed Jesus pouring out "new wine" at Whisper Canyon and in King City—lives are being transformed, and in some cases, the transformations are accompanied by signs, wonders, or miracles. Old Testament prophets used the term "new wine" to describe the joy of Israel's restoration[36] (Joel 2:18-19; Amos 9:13).

In the New Testament, new wine symbolizes the joyful outpouring of the Holy Spirit. On the day of Pentecost recounted in Acts 2, about 120 followers of Jesus were in the upper room when the tangible presence of the Holy Spirit came upon each one of them in a personal and powerful way. But when devout Jews from many different nations overheard mighty works of God being described in their own languages, they thought the disciples were drunk on new wine. Peter quickly explained that they weren't drunk but were filled with the Holy Spirit as the prophet Joel had prophesied (Joel 2:28-32).

As we serve on these outreach trips, we are encountering the Holy Spirit's tangible presence in new and exciting ways. Testimonies of Jesus like those in this book point to the reality that we don't have to wait until we die to experience God's kingdom. Because of Jesus' victory over death, we can experience God's kingdom on earth just like the disciples did long ago.

But Not Everyone Likes New Wine

While this idea of new wine might entice some people to jump barefoot into the wine vat and start crushing grapes, we need to recognize that others might prefer to stay as far away from the winepress as possible. Some of us may have been wounded by overly enthusiastic new wine drinkers who missed the mark. Some may not want to be pushed out of their comfort zones because, frankly, this Holy Spirit thing can be messy. Still, others may put up their guard because they're not sure if it's fake wine or an imposter.

We each have well-founded reasons for our reactions to an outpouring of the Holy Spirit depending on our past experiences, our perception of God, and our theology. Given such a wide range of valid reactions, how are we to respond as the body of Christ to this new wine that's trickling in?

What Did Jesus Say About New Wine?

Let's look at what Jesus said about new wine: "No one puts new wine into old wineskins. If he does, the new wine will burst the skins and it will be spilled, and the skins will be destroyed. But new wine must be put into fresh wineskins...and so both are preserved" (Luke 5:37-38; Matthew 9:17; see also Mark 2:22).

This was Jesus' response to the Pharisees and scribes (Jewish religious leaders) when they asked him why he and his disciples were violating religious traditions and laws. With his disciples in earshot, Jesus used this metaphor to highlight how he was introducing a new way of living, which couldn't be put into the Pharisees' old, rigid mindsets.

These Jewish leaders were ruthless about making people follow God's laws because their ancestors had been forced into exile for disobeying God's laws (2 Kings 17; 2 Kings 24-25; 2 Chronicles 36). To make sure their nation wouldn't be exiled yet again, the Pharisees pressured the Jewish people to live by every letter of the law. Unfortunately, these religious leaders were driven by spirits of fear and legalism.[37]

In contrast, Jesus taught his followers that loving God and loving people is the true essence of God's laws and takes priority over enforcing the letter of the law (Matthew 22:34-40). Throughout his ministry, Jesus poured a new way to live in the Spirit (i.e. new wine) into his disciples. It was the disciples' newly transformed hearts (i.e. fresh wineskins) that allowed them to carry Jesus' new wine. But the Pharisees (i.e. old wineskins) were not able to hold Jesus' new, expansive teachings about God and his kingdom because of their hard hearts.

So what does Jesus' teaching about new wine mean for us today? Given that many believers are uncomfortable with moves of the Holy Spirit, how can we keep our new wine fresh?

Six Practical Ways to Cultivate the Gift of New Wine

Let me offer six practical ways for us to cultivate the gift of new wine Jesus is offering us:

1. Remember what God has done and share your testimonies. I cannot stress this point enough. The Enemy wants nothing more than for us to forget who our loving God is, who we are as his beloved children, and everything he has done for us. In order to overcome the Enemy, it's critical for believers to share what Father God is doing so we can see things from his heavenly perspective rather than allowing ourselves to get buried in discouragement. Notice the blessings of God in your life. Look for stories to celebrate and tell others about God's goodness. (To learn eight ways your testimony can positively impact others, be sure to read Appendix B, "The Life-Changing Power of Sharing Testimonies.")

2. Stay teachable. The Pharisees thought they knew everything there was to know about the Scriptures, but they got a few major things wrong, including the coming of the Messiah.

So, let's be careful not to assume we know everything or that we hear perfectly from God. The Bible says, "our knowledge is partial and incomplete" (1 Corinthians 13:9 NLT). There's always more for all of us to learn, even those in positions of authority and avid studiers of the Word. Let's maintain a life-long-learner attitude and be open to learning more and receiving correction from others so we can continue to grow in the Lord.

3. Discern truth in a community that studies the Bible. Phony miracles from televangelists of the 1960s and 70s made lots of people, including me, doubt moves of God. As a child of the 1960s, I watched those preachers on TV and thought they were as fake as the Big Time Wrestlers. Afterward, I'd play "fake healer" games with my siblings, pretending to be the preacher who prayed and slapped people on the forehead or the person who got knocked out.

Years later, in his ironic humor, God called me into the healing prayer ministry. I've witnessed Jesus cure asthma in minutes, heal incurable diseases over several years, remove pain instantly, heal emotional wounds that have lingered for 30 or 40 years, release trauma, and more.

I now realize Jesus probably did perform true miracles through *some* televangelists, while others were led astray or used healing ministry for personal gain. But rather than dismiss all faith healers and unusual signs and wonders, let's remember what Jesus himself said: "Truly, truly, I say to you, *whoever believes in me* will also do the works that I do; and greater works than these will he do" (John 14:12, emphasis mine).

Jesus also gives us a warning about false prophets. "False messiahs and false prophets will appear. They will work miraculous signs and do wonderful things to deceive, if possible, those whom God has chosen" (Mark 13:22 GW). Four years after I became a born-again believer, I was introduced to the writings of someone who received prophetic messages from God and published them as new revelations from the Lord. Because this prophet performed “real” signs and wonders, I poured out my affections to the Lord, thinking Jesus was behind these miracles and revelations. My husband, Jano, who was not yet a born-again believer, sensed something was wrong and suggested I talk to Brian Morgan, one of our pastors. Brian advised me to check the prophet’s teachings against the Word of God. As I read the Bible, doubts crept in about the writings. I would go to sleep begging God to show me if this was a true or false prophet.

After three months of agonizing, the Holy Spirit confirmed with the Scriptures that the writings were only partially true and that Satan had manifested those “real” signs and wonders, not Jesus. While I was relieved to discover the truth, pain pierced a deep part of my soul because I realized I had allowed Satan to enter the sanctuary of my heart reserved only for Jesus. I felt so stupid for believing the lies. Spirits of shame, self-condemnation, and grief waged war in my mind for months. I am forever indebted to Jano, Brian, and other wise and grace-filled believers who counseled me and prayed for me during that time, and to Jesus who healed those deep wounds.

I share these personal stories with you to stress how important it is to be in a community that supports one another and studies the Word. None of us has all the answers. So when we see something unusual or wonder if it’s really God at work or if it’s a false prophet, let’s spend time asking the Holy Spirit about it and listening for what he has to say.

First Thessalonians 5:19-21 says, “Do not quench the Spirit. Do not despise prophecies, but *test everything*; hold fast what is good” (emphasis mine). Together, let’s discern truth using the whole Bible as our guide. Let’s be a community intent on discussing new wine rather than calling for prohibition. Let's be a people who welcome the kingdom of God on earth, and celebrate the new wine God is giving us by allowing it to breathe.

4. Ask Jesus to give you fresh wineskins by transforming and healing your heart. Every person on the planet has been wounded at one point or another because we live in a fallen world. Sometimes we can be irritated or triggered by things people do because of old wounds that need healing. The good news is, Jesus came to heal the broken-hearted (Isaiah 61:1; Luke 4:18; Psalm 147:3) and he has innumerable ways to do so. I encourage you to release your burdens to Jesus and invite him to transform and heal your heart.

If you're someone who was hurt by a faith healer, false prophet, or a person who misrepresented Jesus, let me first say, I am so sorry that happened to you. I understand the deep pain those types of wounds can cause because I was hurt too. I pray you can forgive the person who hurt you and go to the Lord for healing. Jesus said, "I will never turn away anyone who comes to me" (John 6:37 GW). He longs to heal you of any wounds you may have. Don't let people's mistakes rob you of the spiritual gifts available to you through the Holy Spirit.

5. Ask the Holy Spirit to teach you about spiritual gifts you're not familiar with. We're all part of the body of Christ and we all have different gifts. But we can't be one body of Christ if some parts are missing. I believe the more we learn about *all* the spiritual gifts, the closer we'll come to tasting and seeing the immeasurable greatness, rich fullness, and spiritual completeness God intended for us (Ephesians 1:18-19; 4:11-13).

When we encourage people to steward their gifts and give them the freedom to take risks and make mistakes in a safe learning environment, not only do God's people grow in their spiritual gifting, but everyone in the community benefits as the body of Christ is built up. Being open to all the gifts and relying on the Holy Spirit for guidance in stewarding them expands how God interacts with us, teaches us more about his ways, and allows Christ's light to shine brighter.

Spiritual Gifts in Alphabetical Order

This list was compiled from the following Scripture verses: Romans 12:6-8; 1 Corinthians 12:7-11; 1 Corinthians 12:27-31; Ephesians 4:11; and 1 Peter 4:9-11.

Administration
Apostleship
Discerning spirits
Evangelism
Exhortation
Faith
Generosity
Gifts of healing
Helping
Hospitality
Interpreting tongues
Leadership
Mercy
Pastoring/Shepherding
Prophecy
Serving
Speaking
Teaching
Utterance of knowledge
Utterance of wisdom
Various kinds of tongues
Working of miracles

If you'd like to explore the spiritual gifts you may have, this book is a great resource: "S.H.A.P.E.: Finding & Fulfilling Your Unique Purpose for Life" by Erik Rees. (Zondervan, 2006.)

The Gift of the Holy Spirit

When Jesus rose from the dead and ascended into heaven, he left behind a gift from God freely given to *anyone* who believes in Jesus (John 7:38-39). That gift is the Holy Spirit who lives in the heart of every believer, teaches us to do what's right, guides us into all truth, and helps us stay on the right path (John 16:8; and 16:13). This gift, available through Jesus, is the answer to the Pharisees' law enforcement problem and was prophesied by two Old Testament prophets:

I [the LORD] will put my law within them,
and I will write it on their hearts. —Jeremiah 31:33

I [the LORD God] will... put a new spirit within them.
I will take away their stony, stubborn heart and give them
a tender, responsive heart, so they will obey my decrees and
regulations. Then they will truly be my people,
and I will be their God. —Ezekiel 11:19-20 NLT

Pastor John Piper puts it this way: "The law was kept perfectly by Christ. And all its penalties against God's sinful people were poured out on Christ. Therefore, the law is now manifestly not the path to righteousness; Christ is. The ultimate goal of the law is that we would look to Christ, not law-keeping, for our righteousness."[38] In his last supper sermon, Jesus said, "Loving me empowers you to obey my word. And my Father will love you so deeply that we will come to you and make you our dwelling place" (John 14:23 TPT; see also Romans 8:11).

To receive the gift of the Holy Spirit, invite Jesus to become a bigger part of your life. See Appendix A, "Activate a Stronger Connection with God" for suggested prayers.

6. Practice a new normal. The sixth way to cultivate Jesus' gift of new wine is to be intentional about practicing new ways of encountering God rather than slipping back into old habits. Here are three suggestions: (a) Make time for rest and refreshment. This may be easy for some, but I know from experience how hard this can be in our fast-paced, productivity-focused world. Ask Father God to help you learn to rest in him and ask Holy Spirit what resting in the finished work of the cross might look like for you. (b) Prioritize quiet time with God and quality time with people rather than focusing on getting tasks done. (c) Find a "new-wine buddy" so you can keep each other grounded in biblical truth and encourage each other in your new normal ways of interacting with God.

One Thing to Remember

I'd like to close with one thing for you to remember: If you want to experience more of God's presence in your life, just nurture your relationship with him by hanging out where he hangs out. You don't have to go on a mission trip to encounter his tangible presence—you can experience him right where you are.

Here are a few places where God hangs out:

With the poor, orphans, and widows. Jesus said, "when you [love and care for] the least of my brethren, you do it to Me" (Matthew 25:40). People often sense God's presence when they show love and kindness to those less fortunate than them. Experience more of God by loving those around you.

In your gratitude, appreciation, and praise. Psalm 100:4 says we can enter into God's presence with thanksgiving and praise. Turn your affections toward him and simply appreciate him for what he or others have done for you.

Research shows that expressing our gratitude releases oxytocin in the brain which builds a tight emotional bond with the person you're appreciating.[39] Therefore, the simple act of appreciating God can actually strengthen your connection with him.

In small groups where people feel safe being vulnerable. Join a group where you feel comfortable talking about your faith and how you've experienced God in your life. As Cindi Snedaker said in Chapter 13 on building community, being intentional in receiving one another's stories with grace, acceptance, and unconditional love allows others to encounter Jesus's love through us. That's pretty powerful. Creating safe communities allows people to be transparent—a key to growing in the Lord and being transformed.

On mission trips. Find a mission trip to join so you can discover God in a fresh new way. Getting away from your familiar environment and focusing your attention on loving God and others creates a fertile environment where God can move powerfully.

In summary, simply focusing on loving God and loving people is a great way to experience more of God's presence in your life.

The Continuing Story

This book is just a taste of what God is doing on these mission trips, a small window into the continuing story Jesus is writing in the hearts and lives of PBCC and WGBC volunteers. The children and adults of King City also have their own stories of transformation, which are only hinted about in these pages due to the size and scope of this initial task.

May God bless you abundantly as you ponder these true stories of his extravagant love.

APPENDICES

When I came to you, I did not come
with eloquence or human wisdom
as I proclaimed to you the testimony about God.
My message and my preaching were not
with wise and persuasive words,
but with a demonstration of the Spirit's power,
so that your faith might
not rest on human wisdom,
but on God's power.
—1 Corinthians 2:1, 4-5

Appendix A

Activate a Stronger Connection with God

No matter where you are on your faith journey, God longs for you to step closer to him. Whether you're not sure if he's real, you've been a believer for decades, or you're somewhere in between, there's *always* more to learn about who God is and who we are as his sons and daughters.

If you long to experience more of Jesus' power in your life, I invite you to read one of the following prayers and pray it directly to God. (Feel free to modify as you see fit.)

Prayer to RENEW your connection with God

Lord Jesus,

Thank you for redeeming me through your death and resurrection. I want to experience more of you, Jesus, so I surrender my life to you again. Show me areas I'm trying to manage by myself without your guidance (school, job, finances, health, spouse, children, etc.). Teach me how to release these to you and forgive me for relying on myself and not including you in these areas of my life. Show me what you care about and what you're doing so I can partner with you in your kingdom work here on earth. Help me follow through and obey you. As the author and perfecter of my faith, increase my faith and heal any areas of unbelief. Refresh my spirit, soul, and body so I can follow you even closer. I pray this in the name of Jesus Christ. Amen.

Prayer for GOD TO BECOME REAL

Dear God,

Part of me can see from these true stories that you are a real divine being who wants to have a relationship with me. Another part of me isn't sure you actually exist or care about me because of the way my life has turned out. So God, could you please make yourself real to me? Amen.

Prayer to INITIATE a connection with God

Dear God,

I admit the way I'm running my life apart from you is not working. Forgive me for ways I've hurt myself and others. Thank you for raising Jesus from the dead so I can experience forgiveness and freedom and live with you in eternity. I know that other than believing in Jesus, there's nothing I can do to earn this freedom, so I ask you to be merciful to me and show me your grace. I surrender my life to you now and invite you to change me from the inside. Come into my life in a personal and tangible way. You say in John 10:27 that your sheep hear your voice, that you know them, and they follow you. So please help me hear your voice and help me follow you. Amen.

Behold, I'm standing at the door, knocking.
If your heart is open to hear my voice
and you open the door within,
I will come in to you and feast with you,
and you will feast with me. —Revelation 3:20 TPT

Appendix B

The Life-Changing Power of Sharing Testimonies

Did you know that testimonies actually carry Jesus' resurrection power?

In Revelation 12:11, a loud voice in heaven declares that we, brothers and sister in Christ, actually defeat the Enemy by the blood of Jesus and by sharing testimonies of what he has done in our lives.

Think about that for a minute.

Testimonies are powerful spiritual weapons! Scripture says we can overcome Satan by telling others what Jesus's death and resurrection has done for us.

But exactly how does that work?

Here are eight ways that sharing testimonies can make a life-changing impact on those around you and conquer the Enemy.

1. Testimonies encourage us to put our trust in God rather than in ourselves.

In America, we're used to relying on our abilities and resources, which can make it hard to put our full trust in God. Sometimes it takes an insurmountable situation where we have no other option than to ask God for help. When we see God solve our impossible problems, he reminds us that his ways are so much higher than ours (Isaiah 55:8). So the next time we face a difficult situation, recounting what God did for us in the past reminds us to trust him fully rather than trusting in ourselves.

For example, in 1 Samuel 17:37, young David told King Saul how the Lord had delivered him from the lion and the bear and how God would also deliver him from Goliath. David was relying on the Lord to come through for him again just as he had done in past events in David's life.

The apostle Paul realized the importance of relying on God when he said, "When I came to you, I did not come with eloquence or human wisdom as I proclaimed to you the testimony about God... My message and my preaching were not with wise and persuasive words, but with a demonstration of the Spirit's power, so that your faith might not rest on human wisdom, but on God's power." (1 Corinthians 2:1, 4-5 NIV). When we hear testimonies of God's mighty acts, we discover that no matter how smart we are, relying only on human reasoning is a weak way to address problems compared to God's ways.

2. Testimonies align our thoughts with God's heavenly perspective, lifting us out of our dismal circumstances.

When we hear stories of wonderful things God has done in someone's life, it shatters our old ways of thinking, allows God to break out of the box we put him in, and reminds us that nothing is impossible with him. Testimonies help us look beyond our circumstances and imagine new possibilities. They lift our eyes to the one who can help us, heal us, save us, provide for us, and pull our minds out of self-pity and discouragement. Testimonies align our thoughts with God's heavenly perspective.

King David was a master at crying out to God in his psalms. He starts many of his poems with laments about his stressful circumstances. But when he recounts the Lord's goodness and his mighty deeds, David gains a heavenly perspective, which increases his confidence in the Lord. PBCC Pastor Brian Morgan often teaches a Psalms class where he allows people to give voice to their pain by writing their own psalms. In the process of crying out to the Lord, students in the class gain God's heavenly perspective on their situations, which brings them a profound sense of peace. It's truly remarkable to experience this paradigm shift in our attitudes when we align our thoughts with God's.

3. Testimonies boost our faith in future works of God, giving us hope that he can work in us as he has worked in others.

Sharing testimonies can boost people's faith and cause ripple effects for even more mighty acts of God. In the New Testament, when Jesus healed someone, others would hear about it and crowd around him, hoping to receive healing, too. Several times in his gospel, Matthew says Jesus healed *all* who were sick (Matthew 4:24, 8:16, 9:35, and 14:35-36). Jesus even answered the prayer of a Canaanite woman whose daughter was oppressed by a demon (Matthew 15:21-28).

So when we read stories like the ones in this book, where people experience God in real and tangible ways, we're awestruck. Inspired. True stories of God's work in our lives unveil the resurrection power of Jesus and help us understand the true nature of God and how he loves his people. And when we see him transform hearts and do the miraculous, we can't help but be encouraged that whatever he does for one person, he could do for us, too.

For example, one year when our family was on vacation in Hawaii, we watched a documentary film about miraculous healings done in the name of Jesus. Several people in the film experienced their pain leave immediately after someone prayed for them. When the movie ended, my husband, Jano, allowed me and our three children to pray for God to heal his tailbone. While on a hike the day before, he had fallen on a steep rocky path and bruised it. Right after we prayed for him, the pain left and never returned. We wouldn't have thought to pray for Jano if we hadn't seen the testimonies in the film, which boosted our faith.

4. Testimonies lead others to the Lord.

Sharing our testimonies with others can also have a profound effect on non-believers. For example, when the Samaritan woman told the townspeople how Jesus knew everything about her, many of them came to believe in Jesus simply because of her testimony (John 4:39). When Moses told his father-in-law, Jethro, about all the signs and wonders God had done to Pharaoh and the Egyptians and how God had delivered the Israelites out of bondage, Jethro's response was, "Now I know that the Lord is greater than all gods" (Exodus 18:11).

Jesus himself said to an official whose son was dying, "Unless you see signs and wonders, you will not believe" (John 4:48). The Greek word for "you" in this verse is plural both times it's used,[40] so Jesus was not speaking directly to the official. Although we don't know exactly what group of people Jesus was referring to in this verse, the fact that Jesus healed the man's son shows he was not rebuking the official in this passage. He was simply acknowledging that *sometimes* people need to see God's mighty acts in order to believe. In the same way, our modern-day testimonies of what God is doing in our lives can lead non-believers to Christ by showing them his goodness and power.

5. Testimonies usher us into God's throne room.

Psalm 100:4 tells us that thanking God opens the gates of heaven and praising him ushers us into his throne room, that is, his presence. So when we share stories of what God has done in our lives and thank and praise him in the process, it draws us nearer to God. As our thanksgiving and praise increases, so does our nearness to him. Sharing testimonies with praise and thanksgiving can, therefore, usher us into God's presence.

A beautiful example of this in Scripture is when Mary, newly pregnant with Jesus, went to visit Elizabeth, who had also recently conceived. Before Mary had a chance to tell Elizabeth about her pregnancy, Elizabeth asked, "And why is this granted to me that the mother of my Lord should come to me" (Luke 1:43)? When Mary heard this question, a prophetic testimony of her own story, she broke out in a song of praise, which seems to have elevated her into God's throne room.

Recently, I watched a video testimony on YouTube[41] about Jaxon Taylor (the toddler son of Bethel Music's CEO, Joel Taylor), who was dying from an intestinal problem. Friends and family gathered around Jaxon, praising God for his faithfulness and goodness and crying out for the boy's healing. When Johnathan Helser, a Bethel Music artist, heard Jaxon was dying, a spirit of unbelief shot up in front of him. But also, at that moment, a song[42] began to emerge from deep inside of him to combat that spirit of doubt and fear.

I first heard about the story when Jaxon was in the hospital, so I was one of thousands of people praying for this sweet boy.

Later, when I watched the testimony of Jaxon's miraculous healing unfold in the video, the power of God gripped me, flooding my heart with tears. I was overwhelmed with gratitude to the Lord for saving this child. As I watched and joined in the praise song, I felt the Lord's tangible presence and worshiped God for this incredible miracle.[43] Watching that video testimony ushered me into the presence of God.

6. Testimonies help us understand the magnitude of Christ's love.

When we hear true stories like the ones in this book where people experienced God's presence in tangible ways, we begin to understand the width, length, height, and depth of Christ's extravagant love for us, which Paul mentions in Ephesians 3:14-19. We feel Jesus' love when we hear how God helped Shea overcome shyness (Chapter 4), how he removed Esperanza's pain (Chapter 20), how he spoke clearly to Tommy and nudged him to patch up the relationship with his parents (Chapter 6), how he restored Bella and Daphne's friendship (Chapter 23), and how he graciously replaced the high winds with a gentle breeze (Chapter 14).

These and the other testimonies in this book are all signs of God's great love for us. Each of them is a different facet of the Lord's extravagant love, grace, and mercy for us, his beloved children.

7. Testimonies glorify God, filling the whole earth with his glory.

We were created in the image of God for the purpose of glorifying him (Isaiah 43:7). Ray Stedman, one of the founding pastors of Peninsula Bible Church,[44] says our calling as the body of Christ is to glorify God by demonstrating his love through loving deeds, and telling others how we're being transformed by

Jesus.[45] These are also things Jesus commissioned us to do as his followers (John 15:12; Mark 16:15).

I've been in prayer meetings where testimonies are shared and the audience erupts in standing ovations and shouts of joy. This is a beautiful way of giving God the glory for all he has done.

When we tell others what God has done for us, it shines his light in the darkness "so that all the peoples of the earth may know that the hand of the Lord is mighty" (Joshua 4:24), and so one day the whole earth will be filled with his glory (Psalm 72:19; Isaiah 6:3; Habakkuk 2:14).

In the book of Acts, after the disciples prayed for boldness and were filled with the Holy Spirit a second time, they performed many signs and wonders, were thrown in jail, released, and continued to teach in the temple (Acts 4:29-31, 5:12-21). Scripture says they "filled Jerusalem" with their teaching (Acts 5:28). I imagine they also filled Jerusalem with the glory of God through all the testimonies that were shared. What a simple and beautiful way to glorify God and fill the earth with his glory.

8. Testimonies crush Satan's head.

The devil loves to make us forget what God has done for us. When we forget, it's super easy to doubt God's love for us, his faithfulness, and that he'll provide for us. When we doubt God's goodness, we fall into the Enemy's trap of agreeing with his ideas rather than God's, which causes problems.

For example, once when I experienced a supernatural act of God but didn't share it with anyone, I started to doubt it actually happened. The Enemy taunted me with thoughts like, *that didn't really happen; you just imagined it,* which discouraged me. Agreeing with his ideas made me feel separated from God, Satan's number one agenda. Thankfully, I was not actually separated from God's love (Romans 8:38-39). As I told people what God had done, the spirit of discouragement left.

The thing is, when we do share our God moments with others, we conquer the devil in the seven ways described above:

1. by putting our trust in God instead of ourselves,
2. by aligning our thoughts with God's heavenly perspective instead of being weighed down by our dismal circumstances,
3. by believing a similar miracle could happen again,
4. by leading non-believers to Jesus's love and power,
5. by entering into the Lord's presence,
6. by appreciating the magnitude of Christ's extravagant love for us, and
7. by glorifying God.

I don't know about you, but seeing my situation from God's perspective, getting a faith boost, and entering God's presence makes me so excited to share testimonies all the time so I can experience God in my life even more!

So what are you waiting for? Go share what God has done and is doing in your life.

Then I heard a voice from heaven shout,
"Our God has shown his saving power,
and his kingdom has come!
God's own Chosen One
has shown his authority.
Satan accused our people
in the presence of God day and night.
Now he has been thrown out!
They defeated him
by the blood sacrifice of the Lamb
and by the message of God that they told
people." —Revelation 12:10 CEV; 12:11 ERV

Appendix C

How God Led Me to Write This Book

Two weeks after the 2018 trip, those of us who had served on this outreach project gathered for a King City Memories Night to share highlights of what God had done. About one-fourth of our PBCC congregation attended the event. But because less than ten stories were shared that night compared to the 30 testimonies we heard in Whisper Canyon on the last day of the trip, I drove home afterward feeling we hadn't given God the proper glory he deserved for all he had done.

My heart sank, realizing our church body didn't know how powerfully God had moved on the trip.

The next day while on a prayer walk at Fremont Older, a local park, a thought popped into my head: *Write a short book of testimonies to share with our congregation.*

I liked the idea because it fits with the mission statement God gave me years before—knowing Jesus as healer and making him known through writing and healing prayer. But I wanted to make sure it was God's idea to write this book, not mine. I was already writing a memoir God called me to write, so I knew working on this new book would delay the memoir. So I asked him, "If you really want me to write this book, could you please confirm it?"

That week the Lord gave me three confirmations.

1. **Genuine Thankfulness.** After my prayer walk, I went home and watched an online sermon. As I listened, I discovered the main point of the teaching was to honor the Lord with genuine thankfulness. Because I'd been wanting to give God more glory for all he had done, this teaching felt like confirmation to write this book.
2. **The Word "Obey."** During a quiet time with God the next day, I started to doubt whether I should write this book. In that moment, I heard the word "obey" in my head. It felt like God's still small voice, so I immediately responded, "Okay." I then turned to *The Word For You Today* devotional,[46] which stressed the importance of being a *doer* of the word as well as *obeying* it. That felt like another confirmation.
3. **Youth Pastors Approve.** With those two words from God, I took a step of faith and asked the high school pastors what they thought about my compiling a book of King City testimonies. They both loved the idea and encouraged me to go for it. Their approval felt like a solid endorsement to proceed.

However, later that day I thought about all the work and time it would take to write this book. So I asked God again. *Are you sure you want me to stop writing my other book and work on this one?* Like Gideon, I asked God to give me another sign, a dry fleece (Judges 6:39). I was confident he'd understand my need for another confirmation, but I wasn't so sure he'd actually answer me.

Then a few days later, when I wasn't even thinking about the book, several more confirmations came.

4. "The Offering" Song. While on a long drive to San Luis Obispo with my husband, I plugged my iPhone into the car stereo. Although it was April, a song called "Christmas Offering"[47] started playing even though it wasn't on any of my playlists. My ears perked up as I listened to the artist sing about bringing an offering to Jesus so our Lord can receive what he is due. I knew instantly this was my dry fleece from God.

5. Green Light from God. A few days later, while reading *The Word For You Today* devotional again, I was struck by how relevant the day's entry was for my situation. I highlighted the following words, which felt like another direct word from God about writing the book.

> Courage only waits for one thing: a green light from God. And when God gives the *go*, it's full steam ahead, no questions asked. It's about attacking the problem with whatever ox goad God has given you. It's an all-out assault on the forces of darkness, by deciding to become "salt and light" where God has placed you... It's deciding to take action and become His hands and feet."[48]

I had indeed received a green light from God and from our youth pastors. I'd also been thinking about Revelation 12:11 and how sharing testimonies shines light in dark places, boosts people's faith, and overcomes enemy forces.

6. The Spread of God's Life-Changing Truth. God kept using my trusty devotional to annihilate any doubts that tried to creep into my thoughts about writing this book. The next day, God used it to put one more nail in the coffin of doubt. Here's the part I highlighted that day:

> Jesus said, "You are the salt of the earth" (Mt 5:13 NKJV). So get your saltshaker out and start spreading the life-changing truth of God's Word! Jesus also said, "You are the light of the world" (v. 14 NKJV). There's not enough darkness in the whole world to extinguish the light of one small candle. So let your light *shine*.[49]

As I read this passage, I felt God telling me to shine a light in the darkness by spreading the word about how He's working in and through us in King City.

7. "May the Stories Be Published." Twelve days after the 2018 King City Memories Night, I attended a National Day of Prayer event at PBCC. After the service, I was talking to my friend Jennifer Lewis, who had served with her husband, Larry, as volunteer caretakers of Whisper Canyon for several years. We were recounting the marvelous things God had done. Before I told her I was thinking of writing a book of testimonies, she said, "May the stories be published."

I did a double-take, not sure I'd heard her correctly. "What?" I wanted to make sure she was saying what I thought she was saying. So I asked again, "What stories?"

"The testimonies from King City. May the stories be published."

I was amazed yet again. When I asked Jennifer about this later, she said, "That thought just popped out. You like to write and that's a good way to have the stories told and remembered."

With so many confirmations, I sensed God *really* wanted this book written.

These first-fruits of transformation we have tasted and seen appear to be the beginning of a much larger story God will unfold over time in our church community and in King City. We wait eagerly for his purposes to unfold.

How beautiful upon the mountains
are the feet of him who brings good news,
who publishes peace, who brings good news of happiness,
who publishes salvation, who says to Zion,
"Your God reigns." —Isaiah 52:7

Acknowledgments

It's beautiful to watch the body of Christ come together in unity, both on the mission field and back home, to make Jesus known so his kingdom purposes can be accomplished. Compiling and editing *Cultivating Lifelong Faith* would not have been possible without members of that faithful body rallying together and contributing their gifts to this project.

To all the contributing authors–thank you, thank you, thank you for being willing to share the personal ways God is moving in your lives and what he's teaching you. Thank you for taking the time to talk with me about your stories, for allowing me to probe a bit deeper, and for your patience in my asking you to look at "one more revision!" It was a privilege and joy to work with each one of you.

To my faithful writing partners–Christi Naler, Laurie Kehler, Pat Sikora, and Stephanie Shoquist–I'm so grateful for your writing expertise, spiritual insights, and powerful prayers, which were instrumental in launching this book. Christi, I especially appreciate the hours you labored in love to edit extra pages of this manuscript. You gals rock!

To Ryan Hinn and Brian Morgan—thank you for your support on this project and your invaluable feedback on the manuscript. Your guidance made this book even stronger.

To my PBCC family, faithful prayer warriors, and the PBCC Prayer Team, especially Frank and Kathy Leong, Carol Crouch, June May, and Joan Kerst—I felt your prayers as my fingers raced across the keyboard some days, and as I waited on the Lord other days. Thank you so, so much. I could not have birthed this book without your partnership in prayer.

To my friends from the Mount Hermon Christian Writers Conference who prayed with me or advised me on this manuscript—Jan Kern, Joseph Bentz, Edwina Perkins, Kay Marshall Strom, Kelly Edwards Kirstein, David and Keri Lippman, Steve Laube, Tim Riter, Ken Raney, and Christi McGuire—thank you your enthusiastic support and for cheering me on in my writing and ministry.

To Susie Knepper, a dear friend—thank you for your wonderful work of proofreading and editing this book. I love how God brought us together 38 years ago as freshmen at Stanford when I was just beginning to explore a personal relationship with the Lord, and again now, for my writing debut.

To my parents, Luis and Irma Magaña—I love and admire you both more than words can say. Thank you for raising me in a loving, faith-filled, family-centric home, and for modeling throughout my childhood and beyond how to serve and be like Jesus to those in need.

To my children, Ariana, Niko, and Lucas—thank you for your love, friendship, and support. Niko and Lucas, what a delight to experience King City mission trips with you! Ariana, thank you for your input on how each testimony reflects the gospel message. Niko, thanks for your technical support.

To my husband, Jano—I am so blessed to have you as my life-long companion. Thank you for your advice and help throughout this book-writing journey. Your unwavering support of my ministry often feels like a stable and sturdy boardwalk over a rocky and winding path. I have the utmost love and respect for you and look forward to what and whom the Lord brings into our *sometimes*-empty nest.

To Father God, my King; Jesus, my Healer; and Holy Spirit, my Guide—thank you for redeeming my life and calling me your beloved, royal daughter, for giving me the idea to write this book and confirming it so many times so I'd never doubt it was your idea. Thank you for your nearness to me as I did my best to write what's on your heart. I am overflowing with praise and gratitude for all you have done and are doing to make your tangible love known to your beloved sons and daughters at PBCC, WGBC, in King City, and beyond.

Notes

CHAPTER 1

1. Sean Feucht, Pat Barrett, Ben Hastings. "There is a Name." *Victory* (Live), Bethel Music Publishing, 2019.
2. Bethel Music, *Victory* (Live), Bethel Music Publishing, 2019.
3. Brian Johnson, Ben Fielding, Jason Ingram, Joel Taylor. "Promises Never Fail." *Victory* (Live), Bethel Music Publishing, 2017.
4. Brian Johnson, Phil Wickham. "Living Hope." *Victory* (Live), Bethel Music Publishing, 2019.
5. Claude Ely, Molly Skaggs, Jonathan David Helser, Melissa Helser. "Ain't No Grave." *Victory* (Live), Bethel Music Publishing, 2019.
6. Jenn Johnson, Jason Ingram, Ben Fielding, Ed Cash, Brian Johnson. "Goodness of God." *Victory* (Live), Bethel Music Publishing, 2019.
7. Brian Johnson, Ben Fielding, Matt Crocker, Reuben Morgan. "Victory Is Yours." *Victory* (Live), Bethel Music Publishing, 2019.
8. Cory Asbury, Ran Jackson, Ricky Jackson, Brian Johnson. "Endless Hallelujah." *Victory* (Live), Bethel Music Publishing, 2019.
9. After I heard this word from the Lord about gang members, I discovered that several members of our PBCC church body have been ministering to men who were involved in gangs and are now

imprisoned at the Salinas Valley State Prison in Salinas, CA. Since 2014, PBCC volunteers have been teaching a weekly men's Bible study. They also organize worship services two to three times a year where prisoners hear the gospel message. Many of these inmates have either given their lives to Christ or renewed their commitment to the Lord at these worship services. We give all praise and glory to God for redeeming these men!

10. To find out why this trip moved from Mexicali to King City, be sure to read Ryan Hinn's essay on "The History of PBCC's King City Mission Trip."
11. A testimony is a true story of what God has done in a person's life, which can describe the person's conversion or another experience they had with God.

CHAPTER 2

12. Barna Group, "Church Dropouts Have Risen to 64%—But What About Those Who Stay?" September 4, 2019. https://www.barna.com/research/resilient-disciples/ (Accessed on September 5, 2019.)
13. Dr. Kara E. Powell, Brad M. Griffin, and Dr. Cheryl A. Crawford, "Sticky Faith, Youth Worker Edition: Practical Ideas to Nurture Long-Term Faith in Teenagers." (Grand Rapids: Zondervan Youth Specialties, 2011)
14. Barna Group, "Only 10% of Christian Twentysomethings Have Resilient Faith" September 24, 2019. https://www.barna.com/research/of-the-four-exile-groups-only-10-are-resilient-disciples/ (Accessed on November 20, 2019)
15. David Kinnaman and Mark Matlock with Aly Hawkins, "Faith for Exiles: 5 Ways for a New Generation to Follow Jesus in Digital Babylon." (Grand Rapids: Baker Books, 2019)

CHAPTER 3

16. Signs and wonders in the Bible were used to: (a) demonstrate supremacy over other gods (Exodus 7:11-12; 1 Kings 18:38-39; Luke 24:1-7), (b) demonstrate supremacy over creation (Genesis

1; Joshua 10:12-13; Matthew 8:23-27), (c) help people believe (John 2:23; 20:27; Acts 8:13), (d) protect people (Exodus 14:19-20; Joshua 10:8-11, 2 Chronicles 20:15-23), (e) guide people (Exodus 13:21; Matthew 2:2), (f) heal people (Matthew 8:14-17; Luke 7:21, John 9:3), (g) deliver people (Exodus 14:21-25; Luke 8:1-3; Luke 8:26-36), and (h) manifest God's glory (1 Kings 8:10-11; Luke 2:9; John 2:11).

CHAPTER 12

17. A small group of three to four students volunteered to wake up at 5:30 a.m. to help the cook make breakfast Monday through Friday.

CHAPTER 16

18. Tracy is the same child mentioned in Gail Nordby's story, entitled, "One Small Step Leads to Deep Connections."

CHAPTER 17

19. At that time, Whisper Canyon Christian Camp was owned by Mount Hermon Conference Center. It is now owned and operated by First Baptist Church in Paso Robles, CA.
20. Thermagel is a fire-retardant gel. "Fire-retardant gels are superabsorbent polymer slurries with a 'consistency almost like petroleum jelly.' Used as fire retardants, they can be used for structure protection and in direct-attack applications against wildfires. They are also used in the movie industry to protect stunt persons from flames when filming action movie scenes." From an article titled, "Fire Retardant Gel." Last updated October 4, 2019. *Wikipedia*: *https://en.wikipedia.org/wiki/Fire_retardant_gel* (Accessed on October 5, 2019).
21. A yurt is a circular domed tent covered with skins that are stretched over a collapsible lattice framework. It has a wooden foundation and a wooden floor. Many yurts are also surrounded by a wooden deck, depending on the design.

22. Backfires are fires that are started intentionally in order to create a burned area in the path of a fire, depriving oncoming fires of fuel and stopping them from progressing.
23. "Authorities Determine Cause of Chimney Fire Near Lake Nacimiento." Last updated March 29, 2017. *The Cambrian, San Luis Obispo Tribune: https://www.sanluisobispo.com/news/local/community/cambrian/article141587829.html* (Accessed on November 12, 2018).

CHAPTER 19

24. Pastor Andy Drake, who developed a close relationship with staff members of an orphanage in Mexicali and pastors in the area, went to Mexicali by himself in November of 2008. Andy and Eric Forster continue to lead college students and adults on a yearly outreach program in Mexicali.
25. Whisper Canyon Christian Camp is now owned and operated by First Baptist Church in Paso Robles, CA.

CHAPTER 23

26. Patricia Martin, Tommy Greer. "I'm in the Lord's Army." *Action Bible Songs*. Cedarmont Music, 1995.
27. Ben Cantelon, Tim Hughes. "Happy Day." *Your Love Never Fails*. Jesus Culture Music, 2008. CD/DVD.
28. Barry Blair, Bob Herdman, Will McGinniss, Mark Stuart. "Big House." *Don't Censor Me*. ForeFront Records, 1993. CD.
29. David Leonard, Leslie Jordan. "Called Me Higher." *The Longing No. 3 - EP*. Integrity Music, 2012. CD.
30. John Mark McMillan and Sarah McMillan. "King of My Heart." *You Are the Avalanche - EP*. Lionhawk Records, 2015. CD.
31. Chris Brown, Mack Brock, Matthews Ntlele, Steven Furtick, and Wade Joye. "Here as in Heaven." *Hear As In Heaven (Live)*. Elevation Worship. 2015. CD.
32. Caleb Culver, Cory Asbury, Ran Jackson. "Reckless Love." Bethel Music, 2017. Radio Version - Single.
33. To learn more of what God taught me about uninhibited praise, read my blog post at GabrielaBanks.com entitled, "Learning to

Cheer for God Like I Cheer for My Favorite Sports Team." November 21, 2019.
http://gabrielabanks.com/2019/11/learning-to-cheer-for-god-like-i-cheer-for-my-favorite-sports-team/

34. Jonathan Helser, Joel Case, and Brian Johnson. "No Longer Slaves." Bethel Music, 2015. Radio Version - Single.

CHAPTER 24

35. Barna Group, "Church Dropouts Have Risen to 64%—But What About Those Who Stay?" September 4, 2019.
https://www.barna.com/research/resilient-disciples/ (Accessed on September 5, 2019.) See Chapter 2 for more details on the church dropout rate and how to foster long-term faith in young people.

CHAPTER 26

36. Brian Morgan, "Fasting or Feasting?" Catalog Number 1109. December 7, 1997. *Peninsula Bible Church Cupertino:*
https://pbcc.org/sermon-archive/?sermon_id=475 (Accessed on September 14, 2019).

37. The Pharisees mistakenly saw God as a taskmaster like Pharaoh who enslaved the Israelites for 430 years (Exodus 12:40) and forced them to make more bricks with no straw (Exodus 6:5-9). What they didn't realize is that the real taskmaster is the Enemy, not God. Jesus' work on the cross and victory over death set us free from slavery and sin. "So Christ has truly set us free. Now make sure that you stay free, and don't get tied up again in slavery to the law" (Galatians 5:1 NLT). Like good parents who set proper boundaries and guidelines for their children so they won't get hurt, God's laws are for our benefit, not to burden us but to bless us.

38. John Piper, "How Christ Fulfilled and Ended the Old Testament Regime." February 23, 2005. *Desiring God:*
https://www.desiringgod.org/articles/how-christ-fulfilled-and-ended-the-old-testament-regime (Accessed on September 5, 2019).

39. Rita Watson MPH, “Gratitude Sparks Oxytocin and Love: Study Points to CD38.” February 13, 2014. *Psychology Today: www.psychologytoday.com/us/blog/love-and-gratitude/201402/gratitude-sparks-oxytocin-and-love-study-points-cd38* (Accessed on August 1, 2019).

APPENDIX B

40. See the footnote for John 4:48 in the The Holy Bible, English Standard Version. ESV® Text Edition: 2016. Copyright © 2001 by Crossway Bibles, a publishing ministry of Good News Publishers.
41. Bethel Music. “Raise A Hallelujah (LIVE) - Bethel Music | VICTORY.” January 3, 2019. *YouTube: https://www.youtube.com/watch?v=awkO61T6iok&list=PLfBcaZ6Zqi9W1gBM8hc2ZOo4kQ70g2mlb&index=2&t=0s* (Accessed on February 22, 2019).
42. Jonathan Helser and Melissa Helser. “Raise a Hallelujah.” *Victory*. Bethel Music, 2019. (Live).
43. Bethel Music, “The Power of Praise - The Miracle of Jaxon’s Healing.” February 12, 2019. *YouTube: https://tinyurl.com/yy4ceut7* (Accessed on February 22, 2019).
44. Peninsula Bible Church Cupertino is a church plant from Peninsula Bible Church in Palo Alto.
45. Ray C. Stedman, “Body Life,” Revised and expanded by James D. Denney, (Grand Rapids: Discovery House Publishers, 1972), 37 and 31.

APPENDIX C

46. Bob and Debby Gass, “Treasure God’s Word (5),” *The Word For You Today Daily Devotional* (April 24, 2018), 32.
47. Paul Baloche, “Christmas Offering.” *Christmas Worship.* Integrity Music, 2015. CD.
48. Bob and Debby Gass, “What’s Your Oxgoad?” *The Word For You Today Daily Devotional* (April 29, 2018), 35.
49. Bob and Debby Gass, “Christ Brings Progress to All,” *The Word For You Today Daily Devotional* (April 30, 2018), 35.

About Gabriela Banks

© *Jeanne de Polo Photography*

Gabriela Banks grew up as the youngest of six children in a faith-filled, low-income Mexican family in Dallas, Texas. In 1999, after earning a Ph.D. in education from Stanford University, she encountered God's presence in miraculous and prophetic ways, prompting her to give up her career to follow Jesus. For the first three and a half years of her walk with the Lord, she began learning how to discern and hear God's voice at monthly silent retreats led by Patti Pierce of WellSpring.

Gabriela has been attending Peninsula Bible Church Cupertino since 2001, where she led women's Bible studies and currently serves on the prayer team. Since 2011, she has pursued training for physical and inner healing and is a Qualified HeartSync Facilitator for inner healing with House of Hope Healing Center. Her calling in life is to know Jesus as healer and make him known through healing prayer and writing. She values the combination of strong biblical principles coupled with powerful moves of the Holy Spirit. This is Gabriela's first published book.

Gabriela is the daughter of Luis Magaña of Arandas, Jalisco and Irma Angelica Magaña de la Garza of Monterrey, Nuevo Leon, Mexico. She and her husband, Jano Banks, live in California and have three grown children who pop in and out of their empty nest.

Connect with her on social media:

Website: GabrielaBanks.com

Facebook: Facebook.com/GabrielaMBanks

Instagram: Instagram.com/GabrielaMBanks

Share Your Story

It's amazing how something as simple as a story can be so powerful. Sharing testimonies about ordinary people experiencing extraordinary acts of God can have a powerful life-changing impact on all who hear the stories. It makes sense. After all, modern-day testimonies declare that God's kingdom has come to earth. They bring the ancient Bible to life, demonstrating to the world that Jesus is still alive and at work transforming lives.

If you have a true story about something God did either in King City or on an outreach trips to King City, we'd love to hear it.

Send your testimony to
KingCityTestimonies@gmail.com

We look forward to reading first-person accounts from King City residents as well as more stories of how God has moved in and through volunteers. (Note: If your story includes other people, be sure to get their written permission before sharing it.)

We will not hide them from their children,
but tell to the coming generation
the glorious deeds of the LORD, and his might,
and the wonders that he has done.
...so that they should set their
hope in God. —Psalm 78:3-4, 7

Made in the USA
Monee, IL
28 January 2020